SPECTRUM

Test Prep

Grade 6

McGraw-Hill
Children's Publishing

Columbus, Ohio

Credits:
McGraw-Hill Children's Publishing Editorial/Art & Design Team
Vincent F. Douglas, *President*
Tracey E. Dils, *Publisher*
Phyllis Sibbing, B.S. Ed., *Project Editor*
Rose Audette, *Art Director*

Also Thanks to:
4ward Communications, Interior Production
Jenny Campbell, Interior Illustration

McGraw-Hill
Children's Publishing
A Division of The *McGraw-Hill Companies*

Send all inquiries to:
McGraw-Hill Children's Publishing
8787 Orion Place
Columbus, OH 43240-4027

ISBN 1-57768-666-7

5 6 7 8 9 VHG 07 06 05 04

Table of Contents

About the Tests

What Are Standardized Achievement Tests?

Achievement tests measure what children know in particular subject areas such as reading, language arts, and mathematics. They do not measure your child's intelligence or ability to learn.

When tests are standardized, or *normed*, children's test results are compared with those of a specific group who have taken the test, usually at the same age or grade.

Standardized achievement tests measure what children around the country are learning. The test makers survey popular textbook series, as well as state curriculum frameworks and other professional sources, to determine what content is covered widely.

Because of variations in state frameworks and textbook series, as well as grade ranges on some test levels, the tests may cover some material that children have not yet learned. This is especially true if the test is offered early in the school year. However, test scores are compared to those of other children who take the test at the same time of year, so your child will not be at a disadvantage if his or her class has not covered specific material yet.

Different School Districts, Different Tests

There are many flexible options for districts when offering standardized tests. Many school districts choose not to give the full test battery, but select certain content and scoring options. For example, many schools may test only in the areas of reading and mathematics. Similarly, a state or district may use one test for certain grades and another test for other grades. These decisions are often based on the amount of time and money a district wishes to spend on test administration. Some states choose to develop their own statewide assessment tests.

On pages 5–7 you will find information about these five widely used standardized achievement tests:

- *California Achievement Tests (CAT)*
- *Terra Nova/CTBS*
- *Iowa Test of Basic Skills (ITBS)*
- *Stanford Achievement Test (SAT9)*
- *Metropolitan Achievement Test (MAT)*

However, this book contains strategies and practice questions for use with a variety of tests. Even if your state does not give one of the five tests listed above, your child will benefit from doing the practice questions in this book. If you're unsure about which test your child takes, contact your local school district to find out which tests are given.

Types of Test Questions

Traditionally, standardized achievement tests have used only multiple choice questions. Today, many tests may include constructed response (short answer) and extended response (essay) questions as well.

In addition, many tests include questions that tap students' higher-order thinking skills. Instead of simple recall questions, such as identifying a date in history, questions may require students to make comparisons and contrast or analyze results, among other skills.

What the Tests Measure

These tests do not measure your child's level of intelligence, but they do show how well your child knows material that he or she has learned and that is also covered on the tests. It's important to remember that some tests cover content that is not taught in your child's school or grade. In other instances, depending on when in the year the test is given, your child may not yet have covered the material.

If the test reports you receive show that your child needs improvement in one or more skill areas, you may want to seek help from your child's teacher and find out how you can work with your child to improve his or her skills.

California Achievement Test (CAT/5)

What Is the *California Achievement Test*?

The *California Achievement Test* is a standardized achievement test battery that is widely used with elementary through high school students.

Parts of the Test

The *CAT* includes tests in the following content areas:

Reading
- Word Analysis
- Vocabulary
- Comprehension

Spelling

Language Arts
- Language Mechanics
- Language Usage

Mathematics

Science

Social Studies

Your child may take some or all of these subtests if your district uses the *California Achievement Test*.

Terra Nova/CTBS (Comprehensive Tests of Basic Skills)

What Is the *Terra Nova/CTBS*?

The *Terra Nova/Comprehensive Tests of Basic Skills* is a standardized achievement test battery used in elementary through high school grades.

While many of the test questions on the *Terra Nova* are in the traditional multiple choice form, your child may take parts of the *Terra Nova* that include some open-ended questions (constructed-response items).

Parts of the Test

Your child may take some or all of the following subtests if your district uses the *Terra Nova/CTBS*:

Reading/Language Arts
Mathematics
Science
Social Studies

Supplementary tests include:
- Word Analysis
- Vocabulary
- Language Mechanics
- Spelling
- Mathematics Computation

Critical thinking skills may also be tested.

Iowa Test of Basic Skills (ITBS)

What Is the *ITBS*?

The *Iowa Test of Basic Skills* is a standardized achievement test battery used in elementary through high school grades.

Parts of the Test

Your child may take some or all of these subtests if your district uses the *ITBS*, also known as the *Iowa*:

Reading
- Vocabulary
- Reading Comprehension

Language Arts
- Spelling
- Capitalization
- Punctuation
- Usage and Expression

Mathematics
- Concepts/Estimate
- Problems/Data Interpretation

Social Studies

Science

Sources of Information

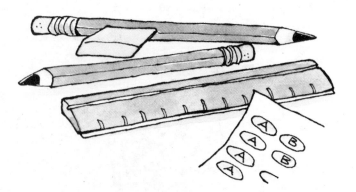

Stanford Achievement Test (SAT9)

What Is the *Stanford Achievement Test?*

The *Stanford Achievement Test, Ninth Edition (SAT9)* is a standardized achievement test battery used in elementary through high school grades.

Note that the *Stanford Achievement Test (SAT9)* is a different test from the *SAT* used by high school students for college admissions.

While many of the test questions on the *SAT9* are in traditional multiple choice form, your child may take parts of the *SAT9* that include some open-ended questions (constructed-response items).

Parts of the Test

Your child may take some or all of these subtests if your district uses the *Stanford Achievement Test*:

Reading
- Vocabulary
- Reading Comprehension

Mathematics
- Problem Solving
- Procedures

Language Arts

Spelling

Study Skills

Listening

Critical thinking skills may also be tested.

Metropolitan Achievement Test (*MAT7* and *MAT8*)

What Is the *Metropolitan Achievement Test?*

The *Metropolitan Achievement Test* is a standardized achievement test battery used in elementary through high school grades.

Parts of the Test

Your child may take some or all of these subtests if your district uses the *Metropolitan Achievement Test.*

Reading
- Vocabulary
- Reading Comprehension

Math
- Concepts and Problem Solving
- Computation

Language Arts
- Pre-writing
- Composing
- Editing

Science

Social Studies

Research Skills

Thinking Skills

Spelling

Statewide Assessments

Today the majority of states give statewide assessments. In some cases these tests are known as *high-stakes assessments*. This means that students must score at a certain level in order to be promoted. Some states use minimum competency or proficiency tests. Often these tests measure more basic skills than other types of statewide assessments.

Statewide assessments are generally linked to state curriculum frameworks. Frameworks provide a blueprint, or outline, to ensure that teachers are covering the same curriculum topics as other teachers in the same grade level in the state. In some states, standardized achievement tests (such as the five described in this book) are used in connection with statewide assessments.

When Statewide Assessments Are Given

Statewide assessments may not be given at every grade level. Generally, they are offered at one or more grades in elementary school, middle school, and high school. Many states test at grades 4, 8, and 10.

State-by-State Information

You can find information about statewide assessments and curriculum frameworks at your state Department of Education Web site. To find the address for your individual state, go to www.ed.gov, click on Topics A–Z, and then click on State Departments of Education. You will find a list of all the state departments of education, mailing addresses, and Web sites.

How to Help Your Child Prepare for Standardized Testing

Preparing All Year Round

Perhaps the most valuable way you can help your child prepare for standardized achievement tests is by providing enriching experiences. Keep in mind also that test results for younger children are not as reliable as for older students. If a child is hungry, tired, or upset, this may result in a poor test score. Here are some tips on how you can help your child do his or her best on standardized tests.

Read aloud with your child. Reading aloud helps develop vocabulary and fosters a positive attitude toward reading. Reading together is one of the most effective ways you can help your child succeed in school.

Share experiences. Baking cookies together, planting a garden, or making a map of your neighborhood are examples of activities that help build skills that are measured on the tests, such as sequencing and following directions.

Become informed about your state's testing procedures. Ask about or watch for announcements of meetings that explain about standardized tests and statewide assessments in your school district. Talk to your child's teacher about your child's individual performance on these state tests during a parent-teacher conference.

Help your child know what to expect. Read and discuss with your child the test-taking tips in this book. Your child can prepare by working through a couple of strategies a day so that no practice session takes too long.

Help your child with his or her regular school assignments. Set up a quiet study area for homework. Supply this area with pencils, paper, markers, a calculator, a ruler, a dictionary, scissors, glue, and so on. Check your child's homework and offer to help if he or she gets stuck. But remember, it's your child's homework, not yours. If you help too much, your child will not benefit from the activity.

Keep in regular contact with your child's teacher. Attend parent-teacher conferences, school functions, PTA or PTO meetings, and school board meetings. This will help you get to know the educators in your district and the families of your child's classmates.

Learn to use computers as an educational resource. If you do not have a computer and Internet access at home, try your local library.

Remember—simply getting your child comfortable with testing procedures and helping him or her know what to expect can improve test scores!

Getting Ready for the Big Day

There are lots of things you can do on or immediately before test day to improve your child's chances of testing success. What's more, these strategies will help your child prepare him- or herself for school tests, too, and promote general study skills that can last a lifetime.

Provide a good breakfast on test day. Instead of sugar cereal, which provides immediate but not long-term energy, have your child eat a breakfast with protein or complex carbohydrates such as an egg, whole grain cereal or toast, or a banana-yogurt shake.

Promote a good night's sleep. A good night's sleep before the test is essential. Try not to overstress the importance of the test. This may cause your child to lose sleep because of anxiety. Doing some exercise after school and having a quiet evening routine will help your child sleep well the night before the test.

Assure your child that he or she is not expected to know all of the answers on the test. Explain that other children in higher grades may take the same test, and that the test may measure things your child has not yet learned in school. Help your child understand that you expect him or her to put forth a good effort—and that this is enough. Your child should not try to cram for these tests. Also avoid threats or bribes; these put undue pressure on children and may interfere with their best performance.

Keep the mood light and offer encouragement. To provide a break on test days, do something fun and special after school—take a walk around the neighborhood, play a game, read a favorite book, or prepare a special snack together. These activities keep your child's mood light—even if the testing sessions have been difficult—and show how much you appreciate your child's effort.

Taking Standardized Tests

No matter what grade you're in, this is information you can use to prepare for standardized tests. Here is what you'll find:

- Test-taking tips and strategies to use on test day and year-round.
- Important terms to know for Language Arts, Reading, Math, Science, and Social Studies.
- A checklist of skills to complete to help you understand what you need to know in Language Arts, Reading Comprehension, Writing, and Math.
- General study/homework tips.

By opening this book, you've already taken your first step towards test success. The rest is easy—all you have to do is get started!

What You Need to Know

There are many things you can do to increase your test success. Here's a list of tips to keep in mind when you take standardized tests—and when you study for them, too.

Keep up with your school work. One way you can succeed in school and on tests

is by studying and doing your homework regularly. Studies show that you remember only about one-fifth of what you memorize the night before a test. That's one good reason not to try to learn it all at once! Keeping up with your work throughout the year will help you remember the material better. You also won't be as tired or nervous as if you try to learn everything at once.

Feel your best. One of the ways you can do your best on tests and in school is to make sure your body is ready. To do this, get a good night's sleep each night and eat a healthy breakfast (not sugary cereal that will leave you tired by the middle of the morning). An egg or a milkshake with yogurt and fresh fruit will give you lasting energy. Also, wear comfortable clothes, maybe your lucky shirt or your favorite color, on test day. It can't hurt, and it may even help you relax.

Be prepared. Do practice questions and learn about how standardized tests are organized. Books like this one will help you know what to expect when you take a standardized test.

When you are taking the test, follow the directions. It is important to listen carefully to the directions your teacher gives and to read the written instructions carefully. Words like *not, none, rarely, never,* and *always* are very important in test directions and questions. You may want to circle words like these.

Look at each page carefully before you start answering. In school you usually read a passage and then answer questions about it. But when you take a test, it's helpful to follow a different order.

If you are taking a Reading test, first read the directions. Then read the questions before you read the passage. This way you will know exactly what kind of information to look for as you read. Next, read the passage carefully. Finally, answer the questions.

On math and science tests, look at the labels on graphs and charts. Think about what each graph or chart shows. Questions often will ask you to draw conclusions about the information.

Manage your time. *Time management* means using your time wisely on a test so that you can finish as much of it as possible and do your best. Look over the test or the parts that you are allowed to do at one time. Sometimes you may want to do the easier parts first. This way, if you run out of time before you finish, you will have completed a good chunk of the work.

For tests that have a time limit, notice what time it is when the test begins and figure out when you need to stop. Check a few times as you work through the test to be sure you are making good progress and not spending too much time on any particular section.

You don't have to keep up with everyone else. You may notice other students in the class finishing before you do. Don't worry about this. Everyone works at a different pace. Just keep going, trying not to spend too long on any one question.

Fill in answer sheets properly. Even if you know every answer on a test, you won't do well unless you enter the answers correctly on the answer sheet.

Fill in the entire bubble, but don't spend too much time making it perfect. Make your mark dark, but not so dark that it goes through the paper! And be sure you choose only one answer for each question, even if you are not sure. If you choose two answers, both will be marked as wrong.

It's usually not a good idea to change your answers. Usually your first choice is the right one. Unless you realize that you misread the question, the directions, or some facts in a passage, it's usually safer to stay with your first answer. If you are pretty sure it's wrong, of course, go ahead and change it. Make sure you completely erase the first choice and neatly fill in your new choice.

Use context clues to figure out tough questions. If you come across a word or idea you don't understand, use context clues—the words in the sentences nearby—to help you figure out its meaning.

Sometimes it's good to guess. Should you guess when you don't know an answer on a test? That depends. If your teacher has made the test, usually you will score better if you answer as many questions as possible, even if you don't really know the answers.

On standardized tests, here's what to do to score your best. For each question, most of these tests let you choose from four or five answer choices. If you decide that a couple of answers are clearly wrong but you're still not sure about the answer, go ahead and make your best guess. If you can't narrow down the choices at all, then you may be better off skipping the question. Tests like these take away extra points for wrong answers, so it's better to leave them blank. Be sure you skip over the answer space for these questions on the answer sheet, though, so you don't fill in the wrong spaces.

Sometimes you should skip a question and come back to it. On many tests, you will score better if you answer more questions. This means that you should not spend too much time on any single question. Sometimes it gets tricky, though, keeping track of questions you skipped on your answer sheet.

If you want to skip a question because you don't know the answer, put a very light pencil mark next to the question in the test booklet. Try to choose an answer, even if you're not sure of it. Fill in the answer lightly on the answer sheet.

Check your work. On a standardized test, you can't go ahead or skip back to another section of the test. But you may go back and review your answers on the section you just worked on if you have extra time.

First, scan your answer sheet. Make sure that you answered every question you could. Also, if you are using a bubble-type answer sheet, make sure that you filled in only one bubble for each question. Erase any extra marks on the page.

Finally—avoid test anxiety! If you get nervous about tests, don't worry. *Test anxiety* happens to lots of good students. Being a little nervous actually sharpens your mind. But if you get very nervous about tests, take a few minutes to relax the night before or the day of the test. One good way to relax is to get some exercise, even if you just have time to stretch, shake out your fingers, and wiggle your toes. If you can't move around, it helps just to take a few slow, deep breaths and picture yourself doing a great job!

Terms to Know

Here's a list of terms that are good to know when taking standardized tests. Don't be worried if you see something new. You may not have learned it in school yet.

acute angle: an angle of less than 90°

adjective: a word that describes a noun (*yellow duckling*, *new bicycle*)

adverb: a word that describes a verb (*ran fast*, *laughing heartily*)

analogy: a comparison of the relationship between two or more otherwise unrelated things (*Carrot is to vegetable as banana is to fruit.*)

angle: the figure formed by two lines that start at the same point, usually shown in degrees 90°

antonyms: words with opposite meanings (*big* and *small*, *young* and *old*)

area: the amount of space inside a flat shape, expressed in square units

article: a word such as *a*, *an*, or *the* that goes in front of a noun (*the chicken*, *an apple*)

cause/effect: the reason that something happens

character: a person in a story, book, movie, play, or TV show

compare/contrast: to tell what is alike and different about two or more things

compass rose: the symbol on a map that shows where North, South, East, and West are

conclusion: a logical decision you can make based on information from a reading selection or science experiment

congruent: equal in size or shape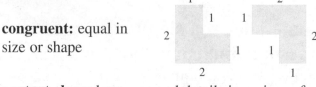

context clues: language and details in a piece of writing that can help you figure out difficult words and ideas

denominator: in a fraction, the number under the line; shows how many equal parts a whole has been divided into ($\frac{1}{2}$, $\frac{6}{7}$)

direct object: in a sentence, the person or thing that receives the action of a verb (*Jane hit the ball hard.*)

equation: in math, a statement where one set of numbers or values is equal to another set (*6 + 6 = 12, 4 × 5 = 20*)

factor: a whole number that can be divided exactly into another whole number (*1, 2, 3, 4, and 6 are all factors of 12.*)

genre: a category of literature that contains writing with common features (*drama, fiction, nonfiction, poetry*)

hypothesis: in science, the possible answer to a question; most science experiments begin with a hypothesis

indirect object: in a sentence, the noun or pronoun that tells to or for whom the action of the verb is done (*Louise gave a flower to her sister.*)

infer: to make an educated guess about a piece of writing, based on information contained in the selection and what you already know

main idea: the most important idea or message in a writing selection

map legend: the part of a map showing symbols that represent natural or human-made objects

noun: a person, place, or thing (*president, underground, train*)

numerator: in a fraction, the number above the line; shows how many equal parts are to be taken from the denominator ($\frac{3}{4}$, $\frac{1}{5}$)

operation: in math, tells what must be done to numbers in an equation (such as add, subtract, multiply, or divide)

parallel: lines or rays that, if extended, could never intersect

percent: fraction of a whole that has been divided into 100 parts, usually expressed with % sign ($\frac{5}{100} = 5\%$)

perimeter: distance around an object or shape

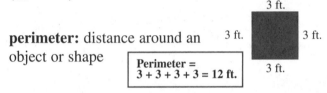

3 ft.

3 ft.   3 ft.

Perimeter =
3 + 3 + 3 + 3 = 12 ft.

3 ft.

perpendicular: lines or rays that intersect to form a 90° (right) angle

90°

predicate: in a sentence, the word or words that tell what the subject does, did, or has (*The fuzzy kitten had black spots on its belly.*)

predict: in science or reading, to use given information to decide what will happen

prefixes/suffixes: letters added to the beginning or end of a word to change its meaning (*reorganize, hopeless*)

preposition: a word that shows the relationship between a noun or pronoun and other words in a phrase or sentence (*We sat by the fire. She walked through the door.*)

probability: the likelihood that something will happen; often shown with numbers

pronoun: a word that is used in place of a noun (*She gave the present to them.*)

ratio: a comparison of two quantities, often shown as a fraction (*The ratio of boys to girls in the class is 2 to 1, or 2/1.*)

sequence: the order in which events happen or in which items can be placed in a pattern

subject: in a sentence, the word or words that tell who or what the sentence is about (*Uncle Robert baked the cake. Everyone at the party ate it.*)

summary: a restatement of important ideas from a selection rewritten in the writer's own words

symmetry: in math and science, two or more sides or faces of an object that are mirror images of one another

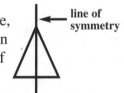

line of symmetry

synonyms: words with the same, or almost the same, meaning (*delicious* and *tasty, funny* and *comical*)

Venn diagram: two or more overlapping circles used to compare and contrast two or more things

square   triangle

• four equal sides
• four 90° angles

• flat shape

• three sides
• three angles

verb: a word that describes an action or state of being (*He watched the fireworks.*)

writing prompt: on a test, a question or statement that you must respond to in writing

Skills Checklists

Which subjects do you need more practice in? Use the following checklists to find out. Put a check mark next to each statement that is true for you. Then use the unchecked statements to figure out which skills you need to review.

Keep in mind that if you are using these checklists in the middle of the school year, you may not have learned some skills yet. Talk to your teacher or a parent if you need help with a new skill.

Reading

❑ I can use context clues to figure out tough words.

❑ I know what synonyms are and how to use them.

❑ I can find words with opposite meanings.

❑ I can tell the difference between a fact and an opinion.

❑ I know the different genres of writing (fiction, nonfiction, etc.)

❑ I can predict what will happen next in a story.

❑ I can paraphrase and summarize what I read.

❑ I can compare and contrast characters and events.

Language Arts

I can identify the different parts of speech.

❑ subject and object pronouns

❑ direct and indirect objects

❑ prepositions

❑ verbs

❑ verb tenses (past, present, and future)

❑ linking verbs

❑ adjectives

❑ adverbs

- ❏ conjunctions
- ❏ prefixes and suffixes

I know how to form negatives correctly.

Writing

Before I write

- ❏ I think about my purpose for writing (to persuade, inform, entertain, describe, etc.).
- ❏ I brainstorm ideas to include in my writing.

When I write a draft

- ❏ I use paragraphs that contain a main idea and supporting details.
- ❏ I use dialogue, action, and descriptive words to tell about my characters.
- ❏ I include details that tell about the setting.
- ❏ I write in different genres.
- ❏ I use reference materials (encyclopedias, dictionaries, the Internet) to find information.
- ❏ I use cause and effect, sequence of events, and other systems to organize my writing.

As I revise my work

- ❏ I check for spelling, capitalization, punctuation, and grammar mistakes.
- ❏ I make sure my paragraphs are well-organized.
- ❏ I add descriptive words and sentences to make my work more interesting.
- ❏ I neatly write or type my final copy.
- ❏ I include my name and a title on the finished work.

Mathematics

Number Sense

I can

- ☐ identify the factors of a number.
- ☐ identify the multiples of a number.
- ☐ use roman numerals.

Addition and Subtraction

I can

- ☐ add and subtract two- and three-digit numbers and greater.
- ☐ add and subtract decimals to the tenths and the hundredths places.

Multiplication and Division

I can

- ☐ multiply two- and three-digit numbers and greater.
- ☐ divide two- and three-digit numbers and greater.
- ☐ divide by one- and two-digit numbers.
- ☐ divide by decimals.
- ☐ multiply and divide by powers of 10.

Measurement

I can estimate and measure using the standard units for

- ☐ length (inch, foot, yard, mile).
- ☐ weight (ounce, pound, ton).
- ☐ capacity (cup, pint, quart, gallon).
- ☐ time (seconds, minutes, hours).

I can estimate and measure using the metric units for

- ☐ length (centimeter, decimeter, meter, kilometer).
- ☐ mass (gram, kilogram).

❏   capacity (milliliter, liter).

I can solve simple problems with units of time, length, capacity, and temperature.

Fractions and Decimals

I can

❏   compare and order fractions.

❏   use the least common multiple.

❏   find prime and common factors.

❏   add and subtract fractions and mixed numbers.

❏   multiply and divide fractions and mixed numbers.

❏   use ratios and proportions.

❏   find percents.

Geometry

I can identify

❏   polygons.

❏   lines, line segments, and rays.

❏   different types of angles, triangles, and quadrilaterals.

I can find the perimeter, area, volume, and circumference of shapes.

Problem Solving

I use different strategies to solve different kinds of problems:

❏   I estimate and use mental math.

❏   I make pictures, diagrams, and charts.

❏   I look for patterns.

❏   I work backwards.

❏   I collect data.

❏   I can read and construct pictographs, line graphs, and bar graphs.

Preparing All Year Round

Believe it or not, knowing how to study and manage your time is a skill you will use for the rest of your life. There are helpful strategies that you can use to be more successful in school. The following is a list of tips to keep in mind as you study for tests and school assignments.

Get organized. To make it easy to get your homework done, set up a place in which to do it each day. Choose a location where you can give the work your full attention. Find a corner of your room, the kitchen, or another quiet place where you won't be interrupted. Put all the tools you'll need in that area. Set aside a drawer or basket for school supplies. That way you won't have to go hunting each time you need a sharp pencil! Here are some things you may want to keep in your study corner for homework and school projects:

- pencils and pens
- pencil sharpener
- notebook paper
- tape
- glue
- scissors
- crayons, markers, colored pencils
- stapler
- construction paper, printer paper
- dictionary

Schedule your assignments. The best way to keep track of homework and special projects is by planning and managing your time. Keep a schedule of homework assignments and other events to help you get organized. Make your own or make a copy of the **Homework Log and Weekly Schedule** provided on pages 22–23 of this book for each week you're in school.

Record your homework assignments on the log as completely as you can. Enter the book, page number, and exercise number of each assignment. Enter dates of tests as soon as you know them so that you can begin to study ahead of time. Study a section of the material each day. Then review all of it the day before the test.

Also make notes to help you remember special events and materials such as permission slips you need to return. List after-school activities so you can plan your homework and study time around them. Remember to record fun activities on your log, too. You don't want to forget that party you've been invited to or even just time you'd like to spend hanging out or studying with friends.

Do your homework right away. Set aside a special time every day after school to do your homework. You may want to take a break when you first get home, but give yourself plenty of time to do your homework, too. That way you won't get interrupted by dinner or get too tired to finish.

If you are bored or confused by an assignment and you really don't want to do it, promise yourself a little reward, perhaps a snack or 15 minutes of playing ball after you've worked really hard for 45 minutes or so. Then go back to work for a while if you need to, and take another break later.

Get help if you need it. If you need help, just ask. Call a friend or ask a family member for help. If these people can't help you, be sure to ask your teacher the next day about any work you didn't understand.

Use a computer. If you have one available, a computer can be a great tool for doing homework. Typing your homework on the computer lets you hand in neat papers, check your spelling easily, and look up the definitions of words you aren't sure about. If you have an Internet connection, you can also do research without leaving home.

Before you go online, talk with your family about ways to stay safe. Be sure never to give out personal information (your name, age, address, or phone number) without permission.

Practice, practice, practice! The best way to improve your skills in specific subject areas is through lots of practice. If you have trouble in a school subject such as math, science, social studies, language arts, or reading, doing some extra activities or projects can give you just the boost you need.

Homework Log
and Weekly Schedule

	Monday	Tuesday	Wednesday
MATHEMATICS			
SOCIAL STUDIES			
SCIENCE			
READING			
LANGUAGE ARTS			
OTHER			

for the week of _____

Thursday	Friday	Saturday/Sunday	
			MATHEMATICS
			SOCIAL STUDIES
			SCIENCE
			READING
			LANGUAGE ARTS
			OTHER

What's Ahead in This Book?

As you know, you will have to take many tests while in school. But there is no reason to be nervous about taking standardized tests. You can prepare for them by doing your best in school all year. You can also learn about the types of questions you'll see on standardized tests and helpful strategies for answering the questions. That's what this book is all about. It has been developed especially to help you and other sixth graders know what to expect— and what to do—on test day.

The first section will introduce you to the different kinds of questions found on most standardized tests. Multiple choice, short answer, matching, and other types of questions will be explained in detail. You'll get tips for answering each type. Then you'll be given sample questions to work through so you can practice your skills.

Next, you'll find sections on these major school subjects: reading, language arts, math, social studies (sometimes called citizenship), and science. You'll discover traps to watch for in each subject area and tricks you can use to make answering the questions easier. And there are plenty of practice questions provided to sharpen your skills even more.

Finally, you'll find two sections of questions. One is called the Practice Test and the other is called the Final Test. The questions are designed to look just like the ones you'll be given in school on a real standardized test. An answer key is at the back of the book so you can check your own answers. Once you check your answers, you can see in which subject areas you need more practice.

So good luck—test success is just around the corner!

Multiple Choice Questions

You have probably seen multiple choice questions before. They are the most common type of question used on standardized tests. To answer a multiple choice question, you must choose one answer from a number of choices.

EXAMPLE	**Cheap has about the same meaning as _____.**

    Ⓐ generous   Ⓒ expensive

    Ⓑ stingy   Ⓓ charitable

Sometimes you will know the answer right away. But other times you won't. To answer multiple choice questions on a test, do the following:

- First, answer any easy questions whose answers you are *sure* you know.
- When you come to a harder question, circle the question number. You can come back to this question after you have finished all the easier ones.
- Eliminate any answers that you know are wrong. The last choice left is probably the correct one!
- Look for clue words like *same*, *opposite*, *not*, *probably*, *best*, *most likely*, and *main*. They can change the meaning of a question or help you eliminate answer choices.

Testing It Out

Now look at the example question more closely.

Think: I know that I'm looking for a synonym for *cheap*. I think that *cheap* means inexpensive or unwilling to spend money. Choice **A,** *generous*, means giving—that's the opposite of *cheap*.

I'm not sure what *stingy* means, so I'll come back to that one. Choice **C,** *expensive*, means "costs a lot." That's also the opposite of *cheap*, so that can't be the answer.

I'm not sure what *charitable* means, but I think it has something to do with charity, which is giving money away. If you give money away, you're not *cheap*, so that's probably not the answer.

Now back to **B,** *stingy*—this is the only remaining choice. I'll try to use it in a sentence in place of *cheap*. "My brother is really *stingy* when it comes to buying birthday presents." Yes, that makes sense. So I'll choose **B,** *stingy*, as my synonym for *cheap*.

Multiple Choice Practice

Directions: Find the word that best completes each sentence.

1 **Artificial** is an antonym for _____.

Ⓐ fake   Ⓒ exquisite

Ⓑ genuine   Ⓓ artifact

2 **Stark** is a synonym for _____.

Ⓕ severe

Ⓖ fancy

Ⓗ starch

Ⓙ true

3 Which word fits best in this group? noun, adjective _____

Ⓐ sticky   Ⓒ adverb

Ⓑ grammar   Ⓓ insect

4 Which word could not fit in this group? barbecue, roast _____

Ⓕ fry   Ⓗ boil

Ⓖ chop   Ⓙ bake

Directions: Read the following passage. Then answer the questions below.

Dr. James Naismith invented basketball in 1891. He was working for a Massachusetts YMCA and his boss asked him to devise a wintertime game that could be played indoors. Then in 1892, Senda Berenson, an instructor at Smith College, adapted Naismith's rules and created women's basketball.

5 Senda Berenson was

Ⓐ a student at Smith College.

Ⓑ a YMCA employee.

Ⓒ an instructor at Smith College.

Ⓓ a friend of Dr. Naismith's.

6 The writer's main purpose is probably to

Ⓕ provide information about basketball history.

Ⓖ entertain readers with a funny story.

Ⓗ convince readers that his or her opinion is right.

Ⓙ persuade readers to support women's basketball.

Fill-in-the-Blank Questions

On some tests you must fill in something that's missing from a phrase, sentence, equation, or passage.

> **EXAMPLE**
>
> **We are regular _____ at La Petite Pastry Shop.**
>
> Ⓐ costumers   Ⓒ characters
>
> Ⓑ customers   Ⓓ guys

To answer fill-in-the-blank questions:

- See if you can think of the answer even before you look at your choices. Even if the answer you first thought of is one of the choices, be sure to check the other choices. There may be a better answer.
- Look for the articles *a* and *an* to help you. Since the word *a* must be followed a consonant and *an* is followed by words starting with vowel sounds, you can often use articles to eliminate choices.
- For harder questions, try to fit every answer choice into the blank. Which makes sense?
- If you get stuck, try filling in the blank on your own choice (not an answer provided). Then look for synonyms for your new word/words among the answer choices.

Testing It Out

Now look at the example question more closely.

Think: Choice **A**, *costumers*, are people who make costumes. That answer doesn't make any sense in this sentence.

Choice **B**, *customers*, makes complete sense; "We are regular *customers* at La Petite Pastry Shop" is the same as saying "we go there often." This is probably the answer, but I'll double-check the others to make sure.

Characters, choice **C**, is also a possibility. "We are regular *characters* at La Petite Pastry Shop." That could mean something like "Everyone knows us there."

Choice **D**, *characteristics*, means "qualities" or "attributes." That choice makes no sense in the sentence.

So back to choices **B** and **C**; although *characters* might fit in that sentence, *customers* fits better, and anyone who reads this sentence would know what it meant. So the answer must be **B**, *customers*.

Fill-in-the-Blank Practice

Directions: Find the word that best completes each sentence.

1 Danny's Pizza Parlor has been in _____ for 20 years.

Ⓐ trouble   Ⓒ school

Ⓑ business   Ⓓ jail

2 The chef uses a secret _____ for his tomato sauce.

Ⓕ receipt   Ⓗ recipe

Ⓖ retreat   Ⓙ gravy

3 His toppings _____ pepperoni, onions, mushrooms, and peppers.

Ⓐ exclude

Ⓑ intrigue

Ⓒ exclaim

Ⓓ include

4 Last week there was an _____ in the newspaper about Danny's.

Ⓕ letter

Ⓖ article

Ⓗ incident

Ⓙ headline

5 The writer _____ the food and service there.

Ⓐ praised   Ⓒ created

Ⓑ prized   Ⓓ ate

6 Her only _____ was that she had to wait a long time for a table.

Ⓕ compliment   Ⓗ compliance

Ⓖ complains   Ⓙ complaint

7 When she set down the pizza, _____.

Ⓐ the waitress said, enjoy your meal!

Ⓑ the waitress said, "Enjoy your meal!

Ⓒ The waitress said, Enjoy your meal!"

Ⓓ the waitress said, "Enjoy your meal!"

8 Danny's won a _____ award last year.

Ⓕ prestigious   Ⓗ important

Ⓖ fastidious   Ⓙ incomparable

True/False Questions

A true/false question asks you to read a statement and decide if it is right (true) or wrong (false). Sometimes you will be asked to write **T** for true or **F** for false. Most of the time you must fill in a circle next to the correct answer.

EXAMPLE **California shares borders with Arizona, Nevada, and Washington.**

Ⓐ true

Ⓑ false

To answer true/false questions on a test:

- First, answer all of the easy questions. Circle the numbers next to harder ones and come back to them later.
- True/false questions with words like *always, never, none, only,* and *every* are usually false. This is because they limit a statement so much.
- True/false questions with words like *most, many,* and *generally* are often true. This is because they make statements more believable.
- Remember that if any part of a statement is false, the entire statement is false.

Testing It Out

Now look at the example question more closely.

Think: I know that California shares a border with Arizona, which is to its east. I know it shares a border with Nevada, which is also to its east. The third name listed is Washington, which I have to assume refers to Washington state because there's no "D.C." shown after. I'm not sure if California shares a border with Washington state. I think that Washington is north of California, but I'm pretty sure that Oregon is the state *directly* north of California. In fact, I have a feeling that Washington state is north of Oregon, not bordering California. So the answer must be **B** for false.

True/False Practice

Directions: Decide if each statement is true or false.

1   **Hawaii lies farther south than Colorado.**

    Ⓐ true   Ⓑ false

2   **Everyone dreams of a Hawaiian vacation.**

    Ⓐ true   Ⓑ false

3   **Some Californians vacation in Mexico.**

    Ⓐ true   Ⓑ false

4   **Alaska is not the largest state.**

    Ⓐ true   Ⓑ false

5   **Montana shares borders with Wyoming and Ohio.**

    Ⓐ true   Ⓑ false

6   **Generally, eastern states are smaller than those in the West.**

    Ⓐ true   Ⓑ false

7   **Vermont is not the smallest state.**

    Ⓐ true   Ⓑ false

8   **Georgia and Tennessee are on the East Coast.**

    Ⓐ true   Ⓑ false

9   **Oregon isn't north of Washington state.**

    Ⓐ true   Ⓑ false

10   **Louisiana is next to Mississippi.**

    Ⓐ true   Ⓑ false

Matching Questions

Matching questions ask you to find pairs of words or phrases that are related in a certain way. You may be asked to draw lines or fill in bubbles to show your answers. The choices are often shown in columns.

Match items that go together.

1	pan	**A**	weigh	**1**	Ⓐ	Ⓑ	Ⓒ	Ⓓ
2	yard stick	**B**	cook	**2**	Ⓐ	Ⓑ	Ⓒ	Ⓓ
3	balance scale	**C**	fasten	**3**	Ⓐ	Ⓑ	Ⓒ	Ⓓ
4	stapler	**D**	measure	**4**	Ⓐ	Ⓑ	Ⓒ	Ⓓ

When answering matching questions on tests, follow these simple guidelines:

- Begin by figuring out the relationship between the two groups of words.
- Match the easiest choices first.
- Try using a difficult word in a sentence. Then repeat the sentence, substituting your answer choices. The answer that fits best in the sentence is probably the correct one.
- Some matching items contain phrases rather than single words. Begin with the column that has the most words. This column will usually give the most information.
- Work down one column at a time. It is confusing to switch back and forth.

Testing It Out

Now look at the example questions more closely.

Think: The first column is a list of tools, and the second column shows what these tools are used for.

A *pan* is usually used to cook, and I see that *cook* is choice **B**.

I think that a *yard stick* is an extra-long ruler. Rulers are used to measure things, and I see that choice **D** is *measure*, so the answer to number 2 is **D**.

I've never used a *balance scale*, but it's probably used like a regular scale is—to weigh things. I see that choice **A** is *weigh*, which is a logical match for *balance scale*.

The last word in the first column is *stapler*, which is used to attach two or more sheets of paper together. The only remaining choice in the second column is *fasten*, which is a synonym for attach. So *fasten* is a good match for *stapler*.

Matching Practice

Directions: For numbers 1–20, match items that go together.

1 1977	**A**	Ronald Reagan	**1**	Ⓐ	Ⓑ	Ⓒ	Ⓓ
2 1981	**B**	George Bush	**2**	Ⓐ	Ⓑ	Ⓒ	Ⓓ
3 1989	**C**	Bill Clinton	**3**	Ⓐ	Ⓑ	Ⓒ	Ⓓ
4 1993	**D**	Jimmy Carter	**4**	Ⓐ	Ⓑ	Ⓒ	Ⓓ

5 Meriwether Lewis	**F**	led slaves to freedom	**5**	Ⓕ	Ⓖ	Ⓗ	Ⓙ
6 Elizabeth Cady Stanton	**G**	scientist and inventor	**6**	Ⓕ	Ⓖ	Ⓗ	Ⓙ
7 Harriet Tubman	**H**	explorer	**7**	Ⓕ	Ⓖ	Ⓗ	Ⓙ
8 George Washington Carver	**J**	advocate for women's rights	**8**	Ⓕ	Ⓖ	Ⓗ	Ⓙ

9 Little Rock	**A**	Ohio	**9**	Ⓐ	Ⓑ	Ⓒ	Ⓓ
10 Springfield	**B**	Arkansas	**10**	Ⓐ	Ⓑ	Ⓒ	Ⓓ
11 Phoenix	**C**	Illinois	**11**	Ⓐ	Ⓑ	Ⓒ	Ⓓ
12 Columbus	**D**	Arizona	**12**	Ⓐ	Ⓑ	Ⓒ	Ⓓ

13 decagon	**F**	eight sides	**13**	Ⓕ	Ⓖ	Ⓗ	Ⓙ
14 pentagon	**G**	ten sides	**14**	Ⓕ	Ⓖ	Ⓗ	Ⓙ
15 rectangle	**H**	five sides	**15**	Ⓕ	Ⓖ	Ⓗ	Ⓙ
16 octagon	**J**	four sides	**16**	Ⓕ	Ⓖ	Ⓗ	Ⓙ

17 $\frac{1}{4}$	**A**	.25	**17**	Ⓐ	Ⓑ	Ⓒ	Ⓓ
18 $\frac{1}{10}$	**B**	0.5	**18**	Ⓐ	Ⓑ	Ⓒ	Ⓓ
19 $\frac{4}{5}$	**C**	0.1	**19**	Ⓐ	Ⓑ	Ⓒ	Ⓓ
20 $\frac{1}{2}$	**D**	0.8	**20**	Ⓐ	Ⓑ	Ⓒ	Ⓓ

Analogy Questions

Analogies ask you to figure out the relationship between two things. Then you must complete another pair with the same relationship.

> **EXAMPLE**   **Meat is to spoiled as bread is to _____.**
>
> Ⓐ rancid   Ⓑ moldy   Ⓒ baked   Ⓓ stale

Analogies usually have two pairs of items. In the question above, the two pairs are *meat/spoiled* and *bread/_____*. To answer analogy questions on standardized tests:

- Find the missing item that completes the second pair. First, figure out how the first pair of items relate to each other. Form a sentence that explains how they are related.
- Next, use your sentence to figure out the missing word in the second pair of items.
- For more difficult analogies, try each answer choice in the sentence you formed. Choose the answer that fits best.
- Decide if you are looking for a noun, verb, adjective, or other part of speech. If the first pair of words are nouns and the word you are looking to match is a noun, you're probably looking for a noun among the answer choices. In that situation, you can eliminate any choices that are not nouns.

Testing It Out

Now look at the example question more closely.

Think: I'll make a sentence out of the first pair: "When *meat* is *spoiled*, you can't eat it." The new sentence I need to complete is "When *bread* is _____, you can't eat it."

Choice **A,** *rancid*, means something like *spoiled*, but I think it only refers to things you drink (like juice.) I've never heard anyone say, "Bread is *rancid*."

If I insert choice **B** into my sentence, I get "When *bread* is *moldy*, you can't eat it." That's definitely true. I'll note **B** as a good choice.

Choice **C** would be "When *bread* is *baked*, you can't eat it." That's not true—bread is usually baked before it's eaten. That choice is wrong.

D would be "When *bread* is *stale*, you can't eat it." Bread is not very tasty when it's stale, but I wouldn't say you *can't* eat it. So **D** is probably not the correct answer. I'll choose **B,** *moldy*, as my answer.

Analogy Practice

Directions: Find the word that best completes each analogy.

1 **Penny** is to **1 cent** as **nickel** is to _____.

Ⓐ dime
Ⓒ 5 cents

Ⓑ 5 dollars
Ⓓ coin

2 **Cat** is to **tabby** as **dog** is to _____.

Ⓕ collie
Ⓗ breed

Ⓖ bark
Ⓙ pet

3 **Chandelier** is to **lamp** as **mansion** is to _____.

Ⓐ Persian rug
Ⓒ fancy

Ⓑ mention
Ⓓ house

4 **Inhale** is to **exhale** as **tense** is to _____.

Ⓕ breathe
Ⓗ gasp

Ⓖ nervous
Ⓙ relaxed

5 **Devastate** is to **destroy** as **renovate** is to _____.

Ⓐ pulverize
Ⓒ replant

Ⓑ create
Ⓓ remodel

6 **Officer** is to **police force** as **soldier** is to _____.

Ⓕ business
Ⓗ army

Ⓖ uniform
Ⓙ commander

7 **Eggs** are to **omelet** as **bread** is to _____.

Ⓐ lunch
Ⓒ cheese

Ⓑ sandwich
Ⓓ wheat

8 **"Thank you"** is to **politeness** as **"shut up"** is to _____.

Ⓕ rudeness
Ⓗ be quiet

Ⓖ no, you shut up
Ⓙ open up

9 **World Wide Web** is to **www** as **United States of America** is to _____.

Ⓐ country
Ⓒ U.S.

Ⓑ U.S.A.
Ⓓ America

10 **Small** is to **petite** as **thin** is to _____.

Ⓕ slender
Ⓗ tall

Ⓖ fat
Ⓙ bony

Short Answer Questions

Some test questions don't have answers to choose from. Instead, you must write short answers in your own words. You must respond to a passage or other information you have been given. These are called "short answer" or "open response" questions.

EXAMPLE

Jade begged her father to let her get a cat, but he worried that she wouldn't take care of it. So Jade worked hard to show how responsible she was. She even took out the trash every night and did all her homework every day after she got home from school.

When Jade's birthday came, she got a board game and some new clothes. Then, at the last minute, her father handed her a shoebox—with a baby kitten inside! This was Jade's best birthday ever.

1. What is the main idea of this passage? _____

2. Do you think Jade will take good care of the new kitten? How do you know?

_____

When you must write short answers to questions on a standardized test:

- Make sure to respond directly to the question that is asked, not details or statements that are given elsewhere in the body of the question.
- Your response should be short but complete. Don't waste time including unnecessary information, but be sure to answer the entire question, not just a part of it.
- Write in complete sentences unless the directions say you don't have to.
- Double-check your answers for spelling, punctuation, and grammar.

Testing It Out

Now look at the example question more closely.

Think: Jade worked very hard to get the kitten and she proved she would care for it by being responsible. So I will write:

1. The main idea of this story is that you can get what you want if you're willing to work hard for it.

2. I think that Jade will definitely take good care of the kitten. She really wanted it, so she showed that she was responsible by helping out in the house and staying on top of her school work. Her parents must trust her if they got her the kitten.

Short Answer Practice

Directions: Read the passage below. Then answer the questions.

Do you think it might be cool to live in outer space one day? Scientists from the United States, Russia, and 14 other countries are way ahead of you. They have been working together for years to build a permanent space laboratory that will orbit the Earth.

When finished, hopefully in 2004, the International Space Station will be home to seven crew members. It will have many of the amenities of modern living, including electricity and running water. The station will contain 52 computers and six laboratories where crew members can perform various experiments. The scientists hope to find out what people need to live in space for long stretches of time. Eventually, they also hope to plan voyages to other parts of outer space.

What is the author's purpose for writing this passage? How do you know?

_____

_____

_____

What is the topic sentence of this passage? _____

_____

_____

In your own words tell why this space station is being built. _____

_____

_____

Would you like to visit the International Space Station some day? Tell why.

_____

_____

_____

_____

_____

Reading

Many standardized tests have sections called "Reading" or "Reading Comprehension." Reading questions test your ability to read for detail, find meaning in a sentence or passage, and use context clues to figure out words or ideas you don't understand.

Here is a list of topics covered on reading tests, along with tips.

Word Meaning

Word meaning questions test your vocabulary and your ability to figure out unfamiliar words. When answering questions about word meaning, do the following:

- Use **prefixes** and **suffixes** to help you understand a word's meaning.

- Use surrounding words to help you guess the meaning of a new word.

Literal and Inferential Comprehension

You will be asked to read short passages and think about their meanings in two ways:

Literal Comprehension: These questions ask about specific details from the story. You can find the answers by going back to the story and reading carefully.

Inferential Comprehension: These require you to draw conclusions or make predictions based on what you've read.

These questions can be harder to answer. If you are not sure about your answers, start by eliminating unreasonable choices.

Main Idea

You will be asked to identify the main idea of some of the passages you read. The **main idea** is the most important idea about a topic or passage. Questions about the main idea might look like this:

What is the main idea of the passage?

What is the writer's purpose?

What would be a good title for this story?

Genre and Style

- You will probably be asked to identify the **genre**, or category, to which a passage belongs. Genre categories include science fiction, fantasy, adventure, persuasive writing, and newspaper articles.

- The way in which writers use words and sentences is called **style**. You may be asked to describe techniques a writer uses. These may include **simile**: a comparison using *like* or *as*; **metaphor**: a comparison of two different objects; and **personification**: a description that gives an object lifelike qualities.

Reading Practice

Directions: Read the passage and then answer the questions.

Fingers of frost tickled at Little Deer's feet. It was a chilly fall morning, but there was no time for Little Deer to snuggle beneath her buffalo skins. It was going to be a busy day, helping her mother to finish the cover for their family's new tipi.

Little Deer slid her tunic over her head and fastened her moccasins. Wrapping herself up in another skin, she walked outside to survey the work they had done so far. The tipi cover was beautiful, and nearly complete. The vast semicircle was spread across the ground, a patchwork in various shades of brown. After her father and brothers had killed the buffalo, she and her mother had carefully cured and prepared the skins, stretching them and scraping them until they were buttery soft. Then with needles from bone and thread made from animal sinew, they had carefully sewn the hides together until they formed a huge canvas nearly thirty feet across.

After they finished the cover today, it would be ready to mount on the lodgepoles. Little Deer's father had traded with another tribe for fourteen tall, wooden poles. They would stack the poles together in a cone shape, lashing them together with more rope made from animal sinews. Then they would carefully stretch the cover over the poles, forming a snug, watertight home. Little Deer smiled in anticipation. She could just imagine the cozy glow of the fire through the tipi walls at night!

1 **How does Little Deer feel about finishing the tipi?**

Ⓐ bored   Ⓒ cold

Ⓑ excited   Ⓓ tired

2 **Which of these statements includes a metaphor?**

Ⓕ Little Deer smiled in anticipation.

Ⓖ Little Deer slid her tunic over her head and fastened her moccasins.

Ⓗ The tipi cover was beautiful, and nearly complete.

Ⓙ Fingers of frost tickled at Little Deer's feet.

3 **This passage would most likely be found in**

Ⓐ an encyclopedia.

Ⓑ a historical novel.

Ⓒ a science fiction story.

Ⓓ a diary.

4 **What is this passage mainly about?**

Ⓕ hunting

Ⓖ building a tipi

Ⓗ being a Native American child

Ⓙ buffalo

Language Arts

Standardized tests usually include sections with questions about spelling, grammar, punctuation, capitalization, and sentence structure. These questions are grouped together in sections called "Language Mechanics and Expression" or "Language Arts."

The following is a list of topics included under Language Mechanics and Expression. Look at the tips and examples that go with each topic.

Grammar

Grammar is the set of rules that helps you write good, clear sentences. Follow these guidelines:

- Remember how to use different parts of speech such as nouns, verbs, adjectives, prepositions, adverbs, and pronouns. Remember that an adjective describes a noun and an adverb describes a verb. Articles (*a, an, the*) are short words that point out specific nouns.

> The tiny puppies burrowed happily under the table.
>
> (article - adjective – noun – verb – adverb – preposition – article – noun)

- A **direct object** is a noun that receives the action of a verb.

> The dog ate the <u>flowers</u>.

- An **indirect object** is a noun that names the person for whom something is done.

> Jamie gave <u>me</u> the flowers.

Capitalization and Punctuation

You will probably be asked specific questions about capitals and punctuation marks, but you will also be required to use them when you write answers in your own words. Keep these points in mind:

- All sentences start with a capital letter, as do all proper nouns.

- Capitalize proper adjectives.

> A <u>C</u>alifornia condor is a beautiful sight to see.

- All sentences should end with a period (.), a question mark (?), or an exclamation point (!). Make sure you pick the one that best fits the meaning of the sentence.

- Use quotation marks around the words that a character says:

> Annie said, "I am so excited about the field trip!"
> "I am, too," added Michele.

Language Arts

- Use apostrophes to show possession or contraction:

  > That is Lila's costume.
  > The girls' uniforms are almost ready.
  > I can't believe you forgot the cake!

Spelling

You may be asked to pick out misspelled words or choose the correct spelling of a word that is already misspelled. You should also check your own spelling when you write.

> The ladys in the club will recieve there membership pins tommorrow. (incorrect)

> The ladies in the club will receive their membership pins tomorrow. (correct)

Sentence Structure

Use complete sentences whenever you write a short answer or paragraph on a test. You may also be asked questions about individual sentences.

Keep in mind the parts of a complete sentence:

- The **subject** is the part of the sentence that is doing something.

  > The delighted fans ran onto the football field.

- The **predicate** is the part of the sentence that tells what the subject is doing.

  > The delighted fans ran onto the football field.

Also keep in mind:

- A **topic sentence** introduces the main idea at the beginning of a paragraph.

- A **concluding sentence** ends the paragraph by summarizing the most important information.

Language Arts Practice

Directions: Choose the set of words with correct punctuation and capitalization. Choose "No mistake" if the underlined part is correct.

1 <u>mr. hopper asked</u> "Have you turned in your homework?"

   Ⓐ Mr. Hopper asked:

   Ⓑ Mr. Hopper asked,

   Ⓒ mr. Hopper asked,

   Ⓓ No mistake

2 My <u>cousins from Akron Ohio,</u> are visiting next week.

   Ⓕ cousins from Akron Ohio

   Ⓖ cousin's from Akron, Ohio,

   Ⓗ cousins from Akron, Ohio,

   Ⓙ No mistake

Directions: Choose the correct word to complete the sentences.

3 I had to run _____ to catch the bus in time.

   Ⓐ quickly

   Ⓑ quicker

   Ⓒ more quick

   Ⓓ quick

4 _____ we were tired from the long trip, we were excited to explore the city.

   Ⓕ Whenever

   Ⓖ Although

   Ⓗ However

   Ⓙ Because

Directions: Choose word that is spelled correctly and best completes the sentence.

5 Ellen was happy to _____ the beautiful gift.

   Ⓐ except

   Ⓑ accept

   Ⓒ axcept

   Ⓓ eccept

6 We used the scales to measure the _____ of the sand.

   Ⓕ wait

   Ⓖ wieght

   Ⓗ weaght

   Ⓙ weight

Language Arts Practice

Directions: Answer the following questions.

7 **What is the complete subject of this sentence? <u>Mona's seven aunts visited her every September.</u>**

Ⓐ Mona

Ⓒ Mona's seven aunts

Ⓑ Seven aunts

Ⓓ aunts visited

8 **What is the simple predicate of this sentence? <u>Amanda and Kirk hiked through the mountains together.</u>**

Ⓔ Amanda and Kirk

Ⓗ through

Ⓕ hiked

Ⓘ through the mountains

Directions: Choose the sentence that is complete and correctly written.

9 Ⓐ Me and Dana practiced our lines for the play.

Ⓑ Maura and I ran the 40-yard dash.

Ⓒ Them and John are part of the school band.

Ⓓ I and her started school last week.

10 Ⓔ Hoped to be first in line, Jane was running.

Ⓕ Mowing the lawn, Jim thinking.

Ⓗ Before she started the car, Blair fastened her seat belt.

Ⓘ Sitting in this class, wondered Alexis.

Directions: Read the paragraph. Then choose the best topic sentence for the paragraph.

11 **All you have to do is fill out an application and bring some mail with your address on it to the library. Then the librarian will enter your information into the computer and prepare your card.**

Ⓐ Have you ever been to the library?

Ⓑ It's easy to get a library card.

Ⓒ Nora loved going to the library.

Ⓓ Joe was proud of his new library card.

Writing

Many tests ask you to respond to a writing prompt. When responding to a writing prompt, follow these guidelines:

Example

What is the most important way that the Internet has changed people's lives? Give at least two examples to support your answers.

The following is a list of guidelines to use when responding to a writing prompt.

Read the Prompt

- Read the instructions carefully. Sometimes you will be given a choice of questions or topics to write about. You don't want to respond to more questions than you need to.

- Once you have located the prompt to answer, read it twice to be sure you understand it. Remember, there is no one right response to a writing prompt. There are only stronger and weaker arguments.

Prewrite

- Before you write your answer, jot down some details to include.

- You may find it helpful to use a chart, web, illustration, or outline to help you organize the information you want to include in your response.

A web is a way of organizing your thoughts. If you were writing about how the Internet has changed people's lives, your web might look like this:

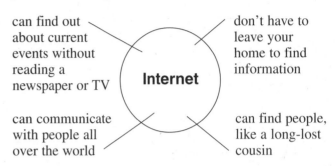

can find out about current events without reading a newspaper or TV

don't have to leave your home to find information

Internet

can communicate with people all over the world

can find people, like a long-lost cousin

- Even if you aren't asked to, it is always a good idea to include facts and examples to support your answer. If the prompt asks you to respond to a reading passage, include specific examples from the passage to strengthen your argument.

Draft

- Begin your answer with a **topic sentence** that answers the prompt and gives the main idea.

- Write **supporting sentences** that give details and tell more about your main idea. All of these sentences should relate to the topic sentence.

- If you are allowed, skip lines as you write. That way you'll have space to correct your mistakes once you're done.

Proofread

- Make sure to proofread your draft for missing words, grammar, punctuation, capitalization, indentation, and spelling. Correct your mistakes.

Writing Practice

Directions: Write a three- or four-paragraph response to <u>one</u> of the questions below.

Think of a character from a book you've read who is *compassionate*. Describe this character and give examples to show how he or she is compassionate.

_____

_____

_____

_____

_____

_____

_____

_____

Do you think there is too much violence on TV, in the movies, and in video games? Give examples to support your answer.

_____

_____

_____

_____

_____

_____

_____

_____

Mathematics: Draw a Diagram

Mathematics Story Problems

Many standardized tests will ask you to solve math story problems. Sometimes these are also called word problems. You have probably already done problems like this in school, so this format will not be new to you. When you see story problems on a test, though, you will have limited time to find your answer.

Use the following strategies to help solve story problems quickly. Remember: not every strategy can be used with every story problem. You will have to choose the best strategy to use for each one.

Draw a Diagram

Sometimes you can draw a diagram to help solve a math problem. Diagrams can help you to see the action of a problem and find a correct solution. Diagrams can often help you solve geometry problems.

A rectangular building is 190 feet long and 158 feet wide. What is the perimeter of the building?

    Ⓐ 32 feet   Ⓒ 696 feet

    Ⓑ 348 feet   Ⓓ 30,020 feet

- Draw your diagram of a rectangle and label the information you are given in the problem. Use the information you are given to determine any other information you need to solve the problem.

- The formula for the perimeter of a rectangle is length + length + width + width, so you need to find the measurements of all four sides of the rectangle.

- Since you know that parallel sides of a rectangle are the same length, you can determine the length and width of every side of the rectangle.

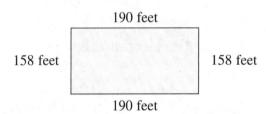

- You can then add the sides together: 190 feet + 190 feet + 158 feet + 158 feet = 696 feet. **B** is the correct answer.

When you draw a diagram:

  ❑ Read the problem carefully.

  ❑ Determine what data you need to solve the problem.

  ❑ Draw a diagram based on the data in the problem.

  ❑ Find how you can use the data in your diagram to solve the problem.

  ❑ Solve the problem.

Diagram Practice

Directions: Draw a diagram to help solve each problem.

1 The rectangular playground measures 45 feet on one side and 32 feet on another side. What is the area of the playground?

Ⓐ 13 square feet

Ⓑ 77 square feet

Ⓒ 1,245 square feet

Ⓓ 1,440 square feet

2 A circle has a diameter of 4 inches. What is the circumference of the circle?

Ⓕ 14 inches   Ⓗ 4 inches

Ⓖ 12.56 inches   Ⓘ 1.27 inches

Formula for circumference:
$C = \pi \times d$ $\pi = 3.14$

3 The Parthenon is 69 meters long, 31 meters wide, and 18 meters high. What is the volume of the Parthenon?

Ⓐ 118 meters   Ⓒ 2,139 meters

Ⓑ 129 meters   Ⓓ 38,502 meters

Mathematics: Trick Questions

Some test questions contain the word *not*. You must be careful to notice when the word *not* is used. These are a type of trick question; you are being tested to see if you have read and understood the material completely.

EXAMPLE **Which number is not equivalent to the mixed number $4\frac{3}{4}$?**

   Ⓐ   4.75

   Ⓑ $4\frac{75}{100}$

   Ⓒ   19/4

   Ⓓ   4.34

- When solving this type of problem, first figure out how the word *not* applies to the problem. In this case you must find the number that is not equivalent to $4\frac{3}{4}$.

- Check the possible answers to see which one is not equivalent to $4\frac{3}{4}$.

    4.75 is the decimal equivalent of $4\frac{3}{4}$.

    $4\frac{75}{100}$ is an equivalent fraction.

    19/4 is $4\frac{3}{4}$ written as a fraction.

    4.34 is *not* equivalent to $4\frac{3}{4}$.

- The correct answer is **D**, since the other choices are all equivalent to $4\frac{3}{4}$.

When you have the word *not* in a problem:

   ☐   Read the problem carefully.

   ☐   Determine what information you need to solve the problem.

   ☐   Compare all of the possible answer choices.

   ☐   Solve the problem.

Trick Questions Practice

Directions: Solve each problem. Remember to look carefully for the word *not*.

1 **Which one of the following shapes may not contain perpendicular lines?**

- Ⓐ a rectangle
- Ⓑ a parallelogram
- Ⓒ a quadrilateral
- Ⓓ an obtuse triangle

2 **Tom measured his closet door and found that it is 46 inches wide. What is the width of his door in feet and inches?**

- Ⓕ 40 feet
- Ⓖ 4 feet, 2 inches
- Ⓗ 4 feet
- Ⓙ 3 feet, 10 inches

3 **Kelli earns $12.50 each week for doing her chores. How much money does Kelli earn in 1 year?**

- Ⓐ $650.50
- Ⓑ $650.00
- Ⓒ $150.00
- Ⓓ None of the above

4 **There are 2,390 students at Ledger School. On field trip day, 1,309 students are going to the park and the zoo. 897 students are going to the dairy farm, and 23 students are going to the hall of science. How many students are not going on any field trip?**

- Ⓕ 2,229 students
- Ⓖ 1,309 students
- Ⓗ 161 students
- Ⓙ All of the above

Mathematics: Paper and Pencil

On tests it often helps to work a problem out using paper and pencil. This helps you to visualize the problem and double-check your answer. It is especially useful when you must solve an equation.

EXAMPLE | **Mackenzie ordered 17 cases of pens. Each case holds 12 boxes and each box holds 48 pens. How many pens did Mackenzie order altogether?** _____

- Here you are not given any answers to choose from; you must figure out the answer using a paper and pencil.

- Use paper and pencil to multiply 17 × 12. This will give you the number of pens.

$$\begin{array}{r} 17 \\ \times\ 12 \\ \hline 204 \text{ boxes} \end{array}$$

- Then use paper and pencil to find the total number of pens in 204 boxes.

$$\begin{array}{r} 204 \\ \times\ 48 \\ \hline 1632 \\ 816\ \ \\ \hline 9{,}792 \text{ pens} \end{array}$$

- There is a total of 1,632 pens. The correct answer is **B**.

When you use pencil and paper:

- ☐ Read the problem carefully.

- ☐ Write neatly so that you do not make errors.

- ☐ Solve the problem.

- ☐ Check your work.

Paper and Pencil Practice

Directions: Solve the problems. Use the work area to show your work.

1 Jupiter has 16 moons. Mars has $\frac{1}{8}$ the number of moons that Jupiter has. How many moons does Mars have?

  Ⓐ 128   Ⓒ 2

  Ⓑ 8   Ⓓ 24

2 What is 3,889 divided by 58?

  Ⓕ 66 R61   Ⓗ 77 R3

  Ⓖ 101 R32   Ⓙ 67 R3

3 What is the area of the rectangle?

  Ⓐ 252 cm

  Ⓑ 32 cm

  Ⓒ 64 cm

  Ⓓ 504 cm

18 centimeters

14 centimeters

4 Andrew earned $5.00 by doing yard work. He added that to some allowance he had saved and bought a new game for $19.78. Then he had $3.22 left over. How much allowance had Andrew saved?

  Ⓕ $14.78   Ⓗ $11.56

  Ⓖ $16.56   Ⓙ $8.22

Mathematics: Guess and Check

One way to solve a word problem is to make your best guess and then word backwards to check your answer.

> **EXAMPLE** **5 less than 3 times Y is 49. What is Y?**
>
> Ⓐ 25   Ⓒ 19
>
> Ⓑ 22   Ⓓ 18

- First, try choosing the most logical answer choice from the choices you have been given. Imagine that your guess for this answer is **C**, 19.

$$19 \times 3 = 57$$
$$57 - 5 = 52$$
$$\text{Check: } 52 > 49$$

- Since your number was too big, you know you should try a smaller number. Guess **D**, 18.

$$18 \times 3 = 54$$
$$54 - 5 = 49$$
$$\text{Check: } 49 = 49$$

- Your guess is correct. $18 \times 3 - 5 = 49$. The correct answer is **D**.

When you use guess and check:

❑ Read the problem carefully.

❑ Make a reasonable first guess.

❑ Revise your guess based on whether your answer was too high or low.

❑ Check that your answer is reasonable based on the question.

Guess and Check Practice

Directions: Use the guess-and-check method to solve these problems.

1 Two numbers have a product of 208 and sum of 34. What are the two numbers?

Ⓐ 17 and 2

Ⓑ 6 and 28

Ⓒ 26 and 8

Ⓓ 25 and 9

2 Michael has been saving money in a jar to buy a new toy. He has $2.42 in bills and coins. If he has 7 bills and coins altogether, which combination of bills and coins does he have?

Ⓕ 2 dollars, 2 quarters, 1 nickel, 2 pennies

Ⓖ 2 dollars, 1 quarter, 2 nickels, 2 pennies

Ⓗ 1 dollar, 3 quarters, 1 dime, 1 nickel, 1 penny

Ⓙ 2 dollars, 1 quarter, 1 dime, 1 nickel, 2 pennies

3 There is a group of pigs and chickens in one area of the barnyard; there are 9 animals in the group. How many of each animal are there if there are 30 animal legs in all?

Ⓐ 6 pigs, 3 chickens

Ⓑ 2 pigs, 7 chickens

Ⓒ 5 pigs, 4 chickens

Ⓓ None of the above

4 Two numbers have a product of 256 and a quotient of 16. What are the two numbers?

Ⓕ 128 and 2

Ⓖ 64 and 4

Ⓗ 32 and 6

Ⓙ 160 and 5

Mathematics: Estimation

Directions: Use estimation to help you narrow down answer choices on a multiple choice test.

> **EXAMPLE**
>
> **The leopard frog can jump up to 91.4 centimeters in a single jump. If a frog jumped 731.2 centimeters altogether, how many jumps did it make?**
>
> Ⓐ 17 jumps   Ⓒ 8 jumps
>
> Ⓑ 12 jumps   Ⓓ 9 jumps

- First, estimate the answer by rounding up or down. Round to the most precise place needed for the problem. In this case, to the nearest one.

  91.4 rounds to 91
  731.2 rounds to 731
  731 ÷ 91 = 8.032

- You can cross off choices **A** and **B** since they are far out of your estimated range.

- Find the exact answer by dividing:

$$91.4 \overline{)731.2} = 8.0$$

- **C** is the correct answer.

When you estimate and answer:

☐ Read the problem carefully.

☐ Round the numbers you need to estimate the answer.

☐ Estimate the answer.

☐ Eliminate any answers not close to your estimate.

☐ Find the exact answer.

Estimation Practice

Directions: Use estimation to solve these problems.

1 14 teachers and 246 students will travel to the Museum of Modern Art. One bus holds 36 people. How many buses are needed altogether?

Ⓐ 2 buses

Ⓑ 7 buses

Ⓒ 8 buses

Ⓓ 12 buses

2 8 friends decide to share the cost of a new telescope equally. If the telescope costs $199.12, how much must each friend pay?

Ⓕ $29.78

Ⓖ $28.25

Ⓗ $24.89

Ⓙ $24.69

3 There are 2,170 monkeys in a nature preserve. They live in groups of 14. How many groups of monkeys are there?

Ⓐ 129 groups

Ⓑ 148 groups

Ⓒ 155 groups

Ⓓ 167 groups

4 Computer headphones cost $12.95. Mrs. Hogan wants to buy 22 pairs of headphones for the school computer lab. How much will it cost to buy the headphones?

Ⓕ $305.90

Ⓖ $284.90

Ⓗ $274.90

Ⓙ $230.85

Mathematics: Incomplete Information

Some test problems may include "Not enough information" as one of the answer choices. When you see a problem with this as an answer choice, watch out! The problem may not contain enough information for you to solve it.

What is the perimeter of this playing field?

Ⓐ 78 feet

Ⓑ 63 feet

Ⓒ 47 feet

Ⓓ Not enough information

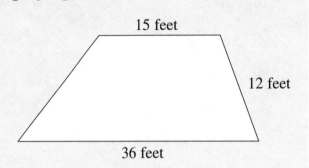

- Determine what information is given in the problem and the picture.
  —the park has 4 sides
  —measurements for 3 sides are given
  —the shape is not a rectangle or square

- Since you do not know the measurements of all 4 sides of the park, you do not have enough information to answer the question.
- Reread the problem to verify that you do not have enough information to solve it.
- Since you do not have enough information, **D** is your answer.

When you think you have incomplete information:

- ❑ Read the problem carefully.
- ❑ Determine what information you need to solve the problem.
- ❑ Check to see if you have all the information to solve the problem.
- ❑ Verify that the information you need to solve the problem is missing.

Incomplete Information Practice

Directions: Solve the problems below.

1 Martin, Collin, and Perry make up 1/9 of the school chorus. How many people are in the chorus all together?

   Ⓐ 12 students

   Ⓑ 27 students

   Ⓒ 54 students

   Ⓓ Not enough information

2 Marla decided to buy 3 toys for her dog. Each toy cost the same amount of money and Marla received $3.12 in change. How much did each toy cost?

   Ⓕ $1.04

   Ⓖ $9.36

   Ⓗ $12.80

   Ⓙ Not enough information

3 Debbie rode her bike to Gwen's house and then home again. It took her 10 minutes to ride there. How far did Debbie ride?

   Ⓐ 10 miles

   Ⓑ 8 miles

   Ⓒ 3 miles

   Ⓓ Not enough information

4 On December 18, James's mom told him he would see his grandmother in 22 days. On what day was James to see his grandmother?

   Ⓕ January 8

   Ⓖ December 40

   Ⓗ January 9

   Ⓙ Not enough information

Mathematics: Using a Calculator

You may be allowed to use a calculator with some standardized tests. Using a calculator can save you time, especially when you need to compute multi-digit numbers. A calculator can also allow you to double-check your work quickly.

EXAMPLE

What is 8^7?

Ⓐ 56

Ⓑ 87

Ⓒ 262,144

Ⓓ 2,097,152

Exponent: the number that tells how may times to use the base number as the factor.

- To solve the problem, you must multiply 8 times 8 seven times. You can do this quickly using a calculator.

$$8 \times 8 \times 8 \times 8 \times 8 \times 8 \times 8 =$$

The correct answer is **D.**

- Be sure to key in the correct numbers to find the correct answer!

When you use a calculator:

❑ Read the problem carefully.

❑ Be sure you key in the correct numbers.

❑ Solve the problem.

❑ Check to see that your answer is reasonable.

Calculator Practice

Directions: Use a calculator to solve the problems below.

1 **78 added to 42^2 is**

- Ⓐ 1,842
- Ⓑ 1,764
- Ⓒ 162
- Ⓓ 120

2 **4^3 plus 9^2 equals**

- Ⓕ 145
- Ⓖ 49
- Ⓗ 40
- Ⓙ 37

3 **The area of a room is 16^2 feet. What is the area of the room?**

- Ⓐ 32 square feet
- Ⓑ 62 square feet
- Ⓒ 256 square feet
- Ⓓ 1,908 square feet

4 **27^3 divided by 9 equals**

- Ⓕ 3
- Ⓖ 47
- Ⓗ 2,187
- Ⓙ 196,683

5 **The population of Centerville is 4×8^4. What is the population of Centerville?**

- Ⓐ 36 people
- Ⓑ 15,893 people
- Ⓒ 16,300 people
- Ⓓ 16,384 people

6 **Some bacteria reproduce by dividing in two. Suppose the number of bacteria in a dish doubles every hour. If there are 2 bacteria to start with, how many will there be after 8 hours?**

- Ⓕ 256 bacteria
- Ⓖ 16 bacteria
- Ⓗ 10 bacteria
- Ⓙ 8 bacteria

Mathematics: Computation

Most standardized tests contain math sections where you must solve a variety of number equations. These questions test your ability to find exact answers to math problems. You will often be allowed to use scrap paper to work out these problems, but the work you show on scrap paper will not count.

The following is a list of skills that are often tested in the Computation segments of standardized tests. The list also contains tips for how to solve tough problems.

Using Operations

Your ability to perform basic mathematical operations (such as addition, subtraction, multiplication, and division) will be tested. Whenever you are solving a math equation, be sure of which operation you must use to solve the problem. Here are some tips:

- Even though you will be given answer choices, it's best to work the problem out first using scrap paper. Then you can compare the answer you found to the choices that are given.

- If you have time, double-check your answer to each problem by using the inverse operation.

- Keep in mind that the same equation may be written differently. Even though these problems look different, they ask you to do the exact same thing. Here are two equations for the same problem:

$$590 \times 32 = ?$$

$$\begin{array}{r} 590 \\ \times\,32 \\ \hline ? \end{array}$$

Other Things to Keep in Mind

- When using decimals, make sure your answer choice shows the decimal point in the correct place.

- Double-check the numerators and denominators of answers with fractions.

- If your problem contains units (such as 2 centimeters + 50 millimeters = X millimeters), be sure the answer choice has the correct units labeled. Many tests will try to confuse you by substituting one unit for another in an answer choice.

- Finally, if you get to a tough problem, use logic to decide which answer choice makes the most sense. Then plug this choice into the equation and see if it works.

Computation Practice

Directions: Find the answer to each problem below.

1   **56.925 − 32.995 =**

    Ⓐ 23.903

    Ⓑ 23.93

    Ⓒ 2.393

    Ⓓ 2.390

2   **8,688 ÷ 12 =**

    Ⓕ 724

    Ⓖ 720.4

    Ⓗ 704

    Ⓙ 624

3   **256 × .99 =**

    Ⓐ 253.44

    Ⓑ 255

    Ⓒ 254.99

    Ⓓ 230.4

4 $\frac{5}{6} + \frac{1}{12} + \frac{1}{3} =$

    Ⓕ $\frac{7}{3}$

    Ⓖ $\frac{11}{12}$

    Ⓗ $\frac{12}{15}$

    Ⓙ $1\frac{1}{4}$

5   **101.2 + 67.02 + 31.09 =**

    Ⓐ 200.31

    Ⓑ 199.31

    Ⓒ 198.31

    Ⓓ 168.22

6   **(15 ÷ 5) + (69 ÷ 3) =**

    Ⓕ 20

    Ⓖ 23

    Ⓗ 26

    Ⓙ None of the above

Mathematics: Concepts

Standardized tests also test your understanding of important math concepts you will have learned in school. The following is a list of concepts that you may be tested on:

Number Concepts

- recognizing the standard and metric units of measure used for weighing and finding length and distance.

- recognizing place value to the millions place and the ten-thousandths place.

- telling time to the minute.

- using a calendar.

- reading a thermometer.

- recognizing prime numbers.

- finding multiples.

- writing and reading expanded notation.

- finding factors.

- calculating to powers of ten.

- finding square roots.

- reading and writing roman numerals.

Geometry

- recognizing parallel and perpendicular lines, rays, and segments.

- identifying solid shapes such as prisms, spheres, cubes, cylinders, and cones.

- finding the area and perimeter of flat shapes.

- finding the area, perimeter, and volume of solid shapes.

- finding the line of symmetry in a flat shape.

- recognizing right, obtuse, and acute angles.

- finding the diameter of a circle.

- recognizing polygons.

Other Things to Keep in Mind

- If you come to a difficult problem, think of what you do know about the topic and eliminate answer choices that don't make sense.

- You may be given a problem that can't be solved because not enough information is provided. In that case, "Not enough information" or "None of the above" will be an answer choice. Carefully consider each of the other answer choices before you decide that a problem is not solvable.

Concepts Practice

Directions: Find the answer to each problem below.

1 **How do you write 119,252 in expanded notation?**

Ⓐ 100,000 + 100,000 + 90,000 + 200 + 52

Ⓑ 100,000 + 10,000 + 9,000 + 200 + 50 + 2

Ⓒ 100,000 + 1,000 + 9,000 + 200 + 50 + 2

Ⓓ 100,000 + 10,000 + 9,000 + 200 + 50 + 2

2 **Which of the following lines are parallel?**

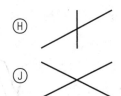

Ⓕ

Ⓖ

Ⓗ

Ⓙ

3 **The square root of 81 =**

Ⓐ 162

Ⓑ 9

Ⓒ 3

Ⓓ None of the above

4 **XVII is the same as which number?**

Ⓕ 13

Ⓖ 8

Ⓗ 17

Ⓙ None of the above

5 **What is the volume of a rectangular prism with a length of 8 feet, a height of 6 feet, and a width of 2 feet?**

Ⓐ 16 cubic feet

Ⓑ 32 cubic feet

Ⓒ 96 cubic feet

Ⓓ None of the above

6 **5 to the third power =**

Ⓕ 25

Ⓖ 125

Ⓗ 625

Ⓙ 1250

Mathematics: Applications

You will often be asked to apply what you know about math to a new type of problem or set of information. Even if you aren't exactly sure how to solve a problem of this type, you can usually draw on what you already know to make the most logical choice.

When preparing for standardized tests, you may want to practice some of the following:

- using a number line with whole numbers and decimals.

- putting numbers in order from least to greatest and using greater than/less than symbols.

- recognizing complex number patterns and object patterns and extending them.

- reading bar graphs, tally charts, or pictographs.

- reading pie charts.

- reading line and double-line graphs.

- reading and making Venn diagrams.

- plotting x-y coordinates.

- finding ratios.

- finding probability.

Other Things to Keep in Mind

- When answering application questions, be sure to read each problem carefully. You may want to use scrap paper to work out some problems.

- Again, if you come to a problem you aren't sure how to solve or a word/idea you don't recognize, try to eliminate answer choices by using what you do know. Then go back and check your answer choice in the context of the problem.

Applications Practice

Directions: Find the answer to each problem below.

1 What is the next number in this pattern? 3, 6, 10, 15, 21, _____

  Ⓐ   25

  Ⓑ   27

  Ⓒ   30

  Ⓓ   None of the above

2 What are the coordinates of point F?

  Ⓕ   (8, 2)

  Ⓖ   (2, 8)

  Ⓗ   (2, 6)

  Ⓙ   (6, 2)

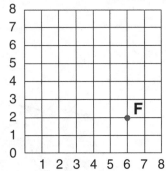

3 If 10 out of 25 students in Mrs. Petrakis's class are going on a field trip, what is the ratio of students who are going to students who are not going?

  Ⓐ   2:5

  Ⓑ   5:2

  Ⓒ   3:2

  Ⓓ   2:3

4 If you put 6 red marbles into a bag and 8 blue marbles into the bag, what is the probability that you'll pull out a red marble on the first try?

  Ⓕ   6 out of 8

  Ⓖ   6 out of 14

  Ⓗ   3 out of 7

  Ⓙ   3 out of 4

5 If you wanted to compare the features of two solid shapes, which would be the best graphic to use?

  Ⓐ   a pie chart

  Ⓑ   a pictogram

  Ⓒ   a Venn diagram

  Ⓓ   None of the above

6 What symbol belongs in the empty box? $\frac{7}{8}$ ☐ 0.9

  Ⓕ   <

  Ⓖ   >

  Ⓗ   =

  Ⓙ   None of the above

Social Studies

Standardized tests often include questions about social studies topics. You may see questions about maps, geography, history, and government.

The following is a list of topics that may be covered on the test and tips to use when solving the questions. Sample questions are also included.

Map Skills

You will probably be asked to look at a map and answer questions about it. Keep these tips in mind:

- All maps include a **compass rose**, a **legend** with **symbols**, and a **scale**.

- **Lines of latitude** (horizontal) and **longitude** (vertical) are the grid lines on maps that help to describe the location of specific places.

- Different maps serve different purposes. There are **political maps**, **physical maps**, **relief maps**, **population maps**, and **topographical maps.**

When you read a map, be sure to read the title first so that you understand the kind of information that is being presented.

Geography

Geography is the study of the land and its features. You should know these terms:

- **natural features:** plateau, mountain, ocean, bay, peninsula, island, isthmus, coastline, butte, cape, delta, dune, strait, mesa, archipelago, atoll, savanna, tributary

- **other geography terms:** hemisphere, equator, prime meridian, continent

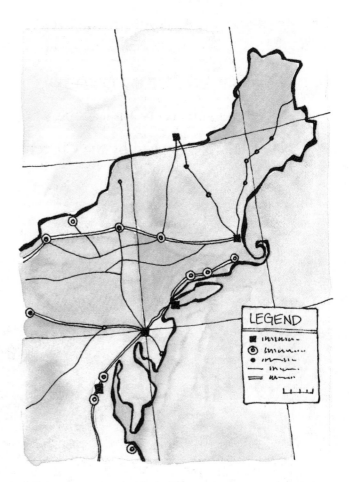

Social Studies

A **time line** organizes historical events in chronological order. Some questions will ask you to use a time line to answer a question.

1. Galileo Galilei sees Jupiter's rings through his telescope 1610	2. Galileo claims that the planets revolve around the sun, not the Earth 1632 3. ? 1633

What is the probable result of the event in 1632?

   Ⓐ Galileo travels to the moon.

   Ⓑ Galileo constructs a telescope.

   Ⓒ Galileo is punished by the Church for his views.

   Ⓓ Galileo travels in time.

The correct answer is **C**. Even if you are not sure of the correct answer, it is easy to eliminate the unreasonable choices: **A**, **B**, and **D**.

Social Studies

Reading Passages

You will probably be asked to read a passage about a social studies topic and to answer questions about it. Keep these tips in mind:

- Before you read, look at the questions first so that you know what kind of information you are looking for.

- Look for key words: *who, what, when, where,* and *why.* These will help you focus on the relevant information in the passage.

- As you read, keep in mind the purpose of the passage: what does the writer want you to learn?

Research Skills

Some questions will test your ability to think like a historian. You will be asked about different sources that historians use to find out historical data. You may need to know:

- different factual sources for doing historical research, like books, encyclopedias, and newspaper articles

- parts of books that help you do research effectively, like a table of contents or an index

Social Studies Knowledge

Some social studies questions will ask specific questions about topics you have been studying in class, such as:

- the Constitution and the Bill of Rights

- the election process and the legislative process

- world religions: Confucianism, Hinduism, Buddhism, Islam, Judaism, and Christianity

- Greek and Roman civilizations

- Mesopotamia and the Fertile Crescent

- Ancient Egypt

As you answer these questions, be sure to make sure you understand what the question is asking. Get rid of the unreasonable answers first, and then make your best guess.

Social Studies Practice

Directions: For questions 1 and 2, study the map and answer the questions.

1 **On what continent would you find Rome?**

Ⓐ South America

Ⓑ Asia

Ⓒ Africa

Ⓓ Europe

2 **Using the scale, about how many miles is it from London to Rome?**

Ⓕ 10

Ⓖ 100

Ⓗ 1,000

Ⓙ 10,000

Directions: Answer questions 3 and 4.

3 **Egypt's leaders were called**

Ⓐ potentates.

Ⓑ emperors.

Ⓒ kings.

Ⓓ pharaohs.

4 **Which of the following is not an artifact?**

Ⓕ a knife

Ⓖ a leaf fossil

Ⓗ a grinding stone

Ⓙ pottery shards

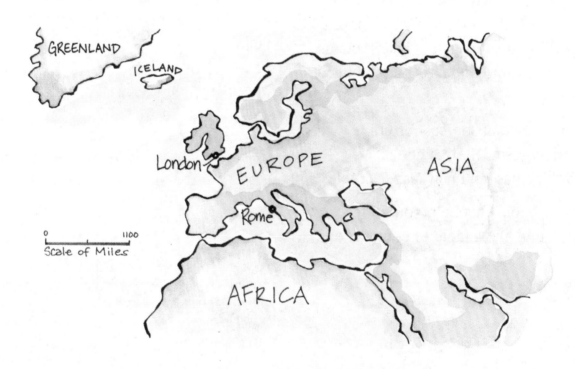

Social Studies Practice

Directions: For questions 5 and 6, read the following passage.

A bill has a long road to travel before it becomes a law. In the beginning, a representative sponsors the bill, and a committee from the House of Representatives examines it to decide if it is worthy. If the committee releases the bill, then it goes to the floor of the House for a vote. If it wins by a simple majority, the bill progresses to the Senate, where a Senate committee examines it. If they decide that the bill should continue, then it goes to the Senate floor for a vote. Again, a simple majority passes the bill. From the Senate, the bill moves to a conference committee, which is made up of members of both the House and the Senate. They agree on any new revisions to the bill, and it is sent back to both the House and the Senate for final approval. After the Speaker of the House and the Vice President sign the bill, it finally moves to the President, who has ten days to sign or veto the bill. If the President vetoes it, the bill can still become a law if both the House and the Senate vote for it by a two-thirds majority.

5 **If a bill is vetoed by the President, it can still be passed if**

  Ⓐ $\frac{2}{3}$ of the Supreme Court votes in favor.

  Ⓑ $\frac{2}{3}$ of the House of Representatives votes in favor.

  Ⓒ $\frac{2}{3}$ of the Senate votes in favor.

  Ⓓ $\frac{2}{3}$ of the House and Senate votes in favor.

6 **Which of the following is the first to vote on a bill?**

  Ⓕ the House of Representatives

  Ⓖ the Senate

  Ⓗ the President

  Ⓙ the Supreme Court

Science

You will often see science questions on standardized tests. These questions may be about scientific facts. They may also test your ability to "think like a scientist." This means you must use data (information) to make predictions and draw conclusions.

The following list of tips includes some words you will need to know. It also contains examples of the types of science questions you may see on a test.

Science Vocabulary

Most science questions will include at least one of the words below:

- **research question:** the question that a scientist asks (*How does sunlight affect plants?*).

- **hypothesis:** A scientist's possible answer to the question (*If there is not enough sunlight, the plants will not grow.*).

- **experiment:** a test to see if the hypothesis is correct.

- **prediction:** a guess about the future results of an experiment (*The plants with more sunlight will be taller than the plants with less sunlight.*).

- **observation:** when a scientist watches the results of an experiment.

- **data:** the information collected in an experiment (*The plant grew 3 inches this month.*).

- **conclusion:** a statement based on information gathered in an experiment (*Sunlight helps plants to grow.*).

- **dependent variable:** an element of the experiment that changes with each different trial.

- **controlled variable:** an element of the experiment that stays the same while other elements change.

Reading Graphs

Standardized tests will often include graphs showing the results of an experiment. You may be asked to read the data on the graph or to use the data to make a prediction or draw a conclusion.

Science

Science Processes

Some science questions will ask you to answer questions about the scientific process. Keep in mind the steps of a scientific experiment and use your common sense as you examine your choices.

A scientist wants to find out how different kinds of plants grow in hot weather. Which variable should she change in each of her trials in order to answer her question?

    Ⓐ the temperature

    Ⓑ the amount of water

    Ⓒ the plants

    Ⓓ the setting

The correct answer is **C** because she is testing the effect of a certain temperature on different kinds of plants. Therefore, each trial should be repeated with a different kind of plant while the temperature remains constant.

Science Knowledge

Science questions on your standardized test may require you to know specific scientific information. This may include information about:

- the living earth (ecosystems, the food chain, renewable and nonrenewable resources)

- atomic structure (atoms and parts of atoms)

- cell structure (parts of cells)

- light and heat (how light and heat travel, conduction and convection)

- heredity (dominant and recessive genes)

If you don't know the answer to a specific question, use your common sense. An excellent strategy is to eliminate unreasonable answers first.

What does a plant produce during photosynthesis?

    Ⓐ oxygen

    Ⓑ carbon dioxide

    Ⓒ water

    Ⓓ salt

In this example, you can easily eliminate **C** and **D** by thinking about what you already know about plants. The correct answer is **A**, because plant respiration is the opposite of human respiration: we inhale oxygen and exhale carbon dioxide, while plants take in carbon dioxide and give off oxygen.

Science Practice

Directions: To answer questions 1 and 2, read the passage.

You have probably heard about Benjamin Franklin's experiments with electricity, but did you know that he was also an inventor of musical instruments? Ben Franklin was interested in sound, and as he conducted various experiments, he invented an instrument called the **glass armonica**. The armonica was just a series of glasses connected together and filled with different amounts of water. The fuller the glass, the higher the note, or **pitch**. As he ran his finger around the rim of each glass, he would produce notes of different pitches and was able to create music!

How did the armonica work? Sound travels in waves: a longer wave will produce a lower pitch, while a shorter wave will produce a higher pitch. A glass that is only filled with a small amount of water has a lot of room left to create a long sound wave—so the glass will produce a low note. A glass that is nearly full has only a little bit of room, so the resulting wave is much shorter, and the note is much higher.

At home, try filling some glass bottles with different amounts of water and then blowing across the top of each bottle. You'll hear sound waves at work!

1 A long sound wave produces a _____ pitch; a short sound wave produces a _____ pitch.

Ⓐ lower; higher   Ⓒ wavy; straight

Ⓑ higher; lower   Ⓓ fuller; emptier

2 One of the glasses in your armonica is producing a note that is too low. How can you make the pitch higher?

Ⓕ place it next to a different glass   Ⓗ pour out water from the glass

Ⓖ add more glasses   Ⓙ add water to the glass

3 Which of the following would not be found in an animal cell?

Ⓐ nucleus

Ⓑ cell membrane

Ⓒ vacuole

Ⓓ chloroplast

4 Materials _____ when heated.

Ⓕ contract

Ⓖ expand

Ⓗ vibrate

Ⓙ travel

Introduction

The remainder of this book is made up of two tests. On page 79, you will find a Practice Test. On page 125, you will find a Final Test. These tests will give you a chance to put the tips you have learned to work. There is also a name and answer sheet preceding each test and an answer key at the end of the book.

Here are some things to remember as you take these tests:

- Be sure you understand all the directions before you begin each test.

- Ask an adult questions about the directions if you do not understand them.

- Work as quickly as you can during each test. There are no time limits on the Practice Test, but you should try to make good use of your time. There are suggested time limits on the Final Test to give you practice managing your time.

- You will notice little GO and STOP signs at the bottom of the test pages. When you see a GO sign, continue to the next page if you feel ready. The STOP sign means you are at the end of a section. When you see a STOP sign, take a break.

- When you change an answer, be sure to erase your first mark completely.

- You can guess at an answer or skip difficult items and go back to them later.

- Use the tips you have learned whenever you can.

- It is OK to be a little nervous. You may even do better.

- After you have completed your tests, check your answers against the answer key. You can record the number of questions you answered correctly for each unit on the record sheet on page 76.

Table of Contents

Name Sheet

Fill in **only one** letter for each item. If you change an answer, make sure to erase your first mark completely. This is a practice name sheet like the ones you will use in school. Follow these directions:

1. Use a No. 2 pencil.

2. Write your name in the boxes. Put only one letter in each box. Then fill in one little circle below each letter that matches that letter of your name.

3. Fill in all the other information.

STUDENT'S NAME				SCHOOL	
LAST		FIRST	MI	TEACHER	
				FEMALE ○ MALE ○	

A name-grid with circled letters A through Z for the LAST, FIRST, and MI name columns.

BIRTHDATE

MONTH	DAY		YEAR
JAN ○	⓪	⓪	⓪
FEB ○	①	①	①
MAR ○	②	②	②
APR ○	③	③	③
MAY ○		④	④
JUN ○		⑤	⑤ ⑤
JUL ○		⑥	⑥ ⑥
AUG ○		⑦	⑦ ⑦
SEP ○		⑧	⑧ ⑧
OCT ○		⑨	⑨ ⑨
NOV ○			
DEC ○			

GRADE

④   ⑤   ⑥   ⑦   ⑧

Record Your Scores

After you have completed and checked each test, record your scores below. Do not count your answers for the sample questions or the writing pages.

Practice Test

Unit 1 Reading
Number of Questions: 28   Number Correct _____

Unit 2 Language Arts
Number of Questions: 43   Number Correct _____

Unit 3 Mathematics
Number of Questions: 33   Number Correct _____

Unit 4 Social Studies
Number of Questions: 18   Number Correct _____

Unit 5 Science
Number of Questions: 20   Number Correct _____

Final Test

Unit 1 Reading
Number of Questions: 26   Number Correct _____

Unit 2 Language Arts
Number of Questions: 41   Number Correct _____

Unit 3 Mathematics
Number of Questions: 35   Number Correct _____

Unit 4 Social Studies
Number of Questions: 10   Number Correct _____

Unit 5 Science
Number of Questions: 7   Number Correct _____

Practice Test Answer Sheet

Fill in **only one** letter for each item. If you change an answer, make sure to erase your first mark completely.

Unit 1: Reading, pages 79–93

A Ⓐ Ⓑ Ⓒ Ⓓ	**6** Ⓕ Ⓖ Ⓗ Ⓙ	**13** Ⓐ Ⓑ Ⓒ Ⓓ	**19** Ⓐ Ⓑ Ⓒ Ⓓ	**25** Ⓕ Ⓖ Ⓗ Ⓙ
B Ⓕ Ⓖ Ⓗ Ⓙ	**7** Ⓐ Ⓑ Ⓒ Ⓓ	**14** Ⓕ Ⓖ Ⓗ Ⓙ	**20** Ⓕ Ⓖ Ⓗ Ⓙ	**26** Ⓐ Ⓑ Ⓒ Ⓓ
1 Ⓐ Ⓑ Ⓒ Ⓓ	**8** Ⓕ Ⓖ Ⓗ Ⓙ	**15** Ⓐ Ⓑ Ⓒ Ⓓ	**21** Ⓐ Ⓑ Ⓒ Ⓓ	**27** Ⓕ Ⓖ Ⓗ Ⓙ
2 Ⓕ Ⓖ Ⓗ Ⓙ	**9** Ⓐ Ⓑ Ⓒ Ⓓ	**16** Ⓕ Ⓖ Ⓗ Ⓙ	**22** Ⓕ Ⓖ Ⓗ Ⓙ	**28** Ⓐ Ⓑ Ⓒ Ⓓ
3 Ⓐ Ⓑ Ⓒ Ⓓ	**10** Ⓕ Ⓖ Ⓗ Ⓙ	**C** Ⓐ Ⓑ Ⓒ Ⓓ	**23** Ⓐ Ⓑ Ⓒ Ⓓ	
4 Ⓕ Ⓖ Ⓗ Ⓙ	**11** Ⓐ Ⓑ Ⓒ Ⓓ	**17** Ⓐ Ⓑ Ⓒ Ⓓ	**D** Ⓐ Ⓑ Ⓒ Ⓓ	
5 Ⓐ Ⓑ Ⓒ Ⓓ	**12** Ⓕ Ⓖ Ⓗ Ⓙ	**18** Ⓕ Ⓖ Ⓗ Ⓙ	**24** Ⓐ Ⓑ Ⓒ Ⓓ	

Unit 2: Language Arts, pages 94–104

A Ⓐ Ⓑ Ⓒ Ⓓ	**11** Ⓐ Ⓑ Ⓒ Ⓓ	**22** Ⓕ Ⓖ Ⓗ Ⓙ	**32** Ⓐ Ⓑ Ⓒ Ⓓ
1 Ⓐ Ⓑ Ⓒ Ⓓ	**12** Ⓕ Ⓖ Ⓗ Ⓙ	**23** Ⓐ Ⓑ Ⓒ Ⓓ	**33** Ⓕ Ⓖ Ⓗ Ⓙ
2 Ⓕ Ⓖ Ⓗ Ⓙ	**D** Ⓐ Ⓑ Ⓒ Ⓓ	**F** Ⓐ Ⓑ Ⓒ Ⓓ Ⓔ	**34** Ⓐ Ⓑ Ⓒ Ⓓ
B Ⓐ Ⓑ Ⓒ Ⓓ	**13** Ⓐ Ⓑ Ⓒ Ⓓ	**24** Ⓕ Ⓖ Ⓗ Ⓙ Ⓚ	**35** Ⓕ Ⓖ Ⓗ Ⓙ
3 Ⓐ Ⓑ Ⓒ Ⓓ	**14** Ⓕ Ⓖ Ⓗ Ⓙ	**25** Ⓐ Ⓑ Ⓒ Ⓓ Ⓔ	**36** Ⓐ Ⓑ Ⓒ Ⓓ
4 Ⓕ Ⓖ Ⓗ Ⓙ	**15** Ⓐ Ⓑ Ⓒ Ⓓ	**G** Ⓐ Ⓑ Ⓒ Ⓓ	**37** Ⓕ Ⓖ Ⓗ Ⓙ
5 Ⓐ Ⓑ Ⓒ Ⓓ	**16** Ⓕ Ⓖ Ⓗ Ⓙ	**26** Ⓐ Ⓑ Ⓒ Ⓓ	**38** Ⓐ Ⓑ Ⓒ Ⓓ
6 Ⓕ Ⓖ Ⓗ Ⓙ	**17** Ⓐ Ⓑ Ⓒ Ⓓ	**27** Ⓕ Ⓖ Ⓗ Ⓙ	**39** Ⓕ Ⓖ Ⓗ Ⓙ
7 Ⓐ Ⓑ Ⓒ Ⓓ	**18** Ⓕ Ⓖ Ⓗ Ⓙ	**H** Ⓐ Ⓑ Ⓒ Ⓓ Ⓔ	**40** Ⓐ Ⓑ Ⓒ Ⓓ
8 Ⓕ Ⓖ Ⓗ Ⓙ	**19** Ⓐ Ⓑ Ⓒ Ⓓ	**28** Ⓐ Ⓑ Ⓒ Ⓓ	**41** Ⓕ Ⓖ Ⓗ Ⓙ Ⓚ
9 Ⓐ Ⓑ Ⓒ Ⓓ	**20** Ⓕ Ⓖ Ⓗ Ⓙ	**29** Ⓕ Ⓖ Ⓗ Ⓙ	**42** Ⓐ Ⓑ Ⓒ Ⓓ Ⓔ
10 Ⓕ Ⓖ Ⓗ Ⓙ	**E** Ⓐ Ⓑ Ⓒ Ⓓ	**30** Ⓐ Ⓑ Ⓒ Ⓓ	**43** Ⓕ Ⓖ Ⓗ Ⓙ Ⓚ
C Ⓐ Ⓑ Ⓒ Ⓓ	**21** Ⓐ Ⓑ Ⓒ Ⓓ	**31** Ⓕ Ⓖ Ⓗ Ⓙ	

Practice Test Answer Sheet

Unit 3: Mathematics, pages 105–114

A Ⓐ Ⓑ Ⓒ Ⓓ Ⓔ   8 Ⓕ Ⓖ Ⓗ Ⓙ   17 Ⓐ Ⓑ Ⓒ Ⓓ Ⓔ   26 Ⓐ Ⓑ Ⓒ Ⓓ

B Ⓕ Ⓖ Ⓗ Ⓙ Ⓚ   9 Ⓐ Ⓑ Ⓒ Ⓓ   18 Ⓕ Ⓖ Ⓗ Ⓙ Ⓚ   27 Ⓕ Ⓖ Ⓗ Ⓙ

1 Ⓐ Ⓑ Ⓒ Ⓓ Ⓔ   10 Ⓕ Ⓖ Ⓗ Ⓙ   19 Ⓐ Ⓑ Ⓒ Ⓓ Ⓔ   28 Ⓐ Ⓑ Ⓒ Ⓓ

2 Ⓕ Ⓖ Ⓗ Ⓙ Ⓚ   11 Ⓐ Ⓑ Ⓒ Ⓓ   20 Ⓕ Ⓖ Ⓗ Ⓙ Ⓚ   29 Ⓕ Ⓖ Ⓗ Ⓙ

3 Ⓐ Ⓑ Ⓒ Ⓓ Ⓔ   12 Ⓕ Ⓖ Ⓗ Ⓙ   21 Ⓐ Ⓑ Ⓒ Ⓓ Ⓔ   30 Ⓐ Ⓑ Ⓒ Ⓓ

4 Ⓕ Ⓖ Ⓗ Ⓙ Ⓚ   13 Ⓐ Ⓑ Ⓒ Ⓓ   E Ⓐ Ⓑ Ⓒ Ⓓ   31 Ⓕ Ⓖ Ⓗ Ⓙ

C Ⓐ Ⓑ Ⓒ Ⓓ   14 Ⓕ Ⓖ Ⓗ Ⓙ   22 Ⓐ Ⓑ Ⓒ Ⓓ   32 Ⓐ Ⓑ Ⓒ Ⓓ

5 Ⓐ Ⓑ Ⓒ Ⓓ   15 Ⓐ Ⓑ Ⓒ Ⓓ   23 Ⓕ Ⓖ Ⓗ Ⓙ   33 Ⓕ Ⓖ Ⓗ Ⓙ

6 Ⓕ Ⓖ Ⓗ Ⓙ   16 Ⓕ Ⓖ Ⓗ Ⓙ   24 Ⓐ Ⓑ Ⓒ Ⓓ

7 Ⓐ Ⓑ Ⓒ Ⓓ   D Ⓐ Ⓑ Ⓒ Ⓓ Ⓔ   25 Ⓕ Ⓖ Ⓗ Ⓙ

Unit 4: Social Studies, pages 115–118

1 Ⓐ Ⓑ Ⓒ Ⓓ   5 Ⓐ Ⓑ Ⓒ Ⓓ   9 Ⓐ Ⓑ Ⓒ Ⓓ   13 Ⓐ Ⓑ Ⓒ Ⓓ   17 Ⓐ Ⓑ Ⓒ Ⓓ

2 Ⓕ Ⓖ Ⓗ Ⓙ   6 Ⓕ Ⓖ Ⓗ Ⓙ   10 Ⓕ Ⓖ Ⓗ Ⓙ   14 Ⓕ Ⓖ Ⓗ Ⓙ   18 Ⓕ Ⓖ Ⓗ Ⓙ

3 Ⓐ Ⓑ Ⓒ Ⓓ   7 Ⓐ Ⓑ Ⓒ Ⓓ   11 Ⓐ Ⓑ Ⓒ Ⓓ   15 Ⓐ Ⓑ Ⓒ Ⓓ

4 Ⓕ Ⓖ Ⓗ Ⓙ   8 Ⓕ Ⓖ Ⓗ Ⓙ   12 Ⓕ Ⓖ Ⓗ Ⓙ   16 Ⓕ Ⓖ Ⓗ Ⓙ

Unit 5: Science, pages 119–122

1 Ⓐ Ⓑ Ⓒ Ⓓ   5 Ⓐ Ⓑ Ⓒ Ⓓ   9 Ⓐ Ⓑ Ⓒ Ⓓ   13 Ⓐ Ⓑ Ⓒ Ⓓ   17 Ⓐ Ⓑ Ⓒ Ⓓ

2 Ⓕ Ⓖ Ⓗ Ⓙ   6 Ⓕ Ⓖ Ⓗ Ⓙ   10 Ⓕ Ⓖ Ⓗ Ⓙ   14 Ⓕ Ⓖ Ⓗ Ⓙ   18 Ⓕ Ⓖ Ⓗ Ⓙ

3 Ⓐ Ⓑ Ⓒ Ⓓ   7 Ⓐ Ⓑ Ⓒ Ⓓ   11 Ⓐ Ⓑ Ⓒ Ⓓ   15 Ⓐ Ⓑ Ⓒ Ⓓ   19 Ⓐ Ⓑ Ⓒ Ⓓ

4 Ⓕ Ⓖ Ⓗ Ⓙ   8 Ⓕ Ⓖ Ⓗ Ⓙ   12 Ⓕ Ⓖ Ⓗ Ⓙ   16 Ⓕ Ⓖ Ⓗ Ⓙ   20 Ⓕ Ⓖ Ⓗ Ⓙ

Reading

Lesson 1 Reading Nonfiction

Directions: Read the following paragraph. Then answer the question.

SAMPLE A

The golden retriever is a popular breed of dog. Mature goldens are large, but their pleasant disposition makes them wonderful family pets. To learn more about golden retrievers, which of these would be most helpful?

A *The History of Dogs*   **C** *The Small Dog Handbook*

B *Training Your Dog*   **D** *The Dog Encyclopedia*

SAMPLE B

Directions: For the following sentence, choose the word that means golden retrievers get along well with children.

Golden retrievers _____ children well.

F display   **H** reject

G tolerate   **J** manipulate

Don't spend too much time reading the story. Just skim it, then skim the questions.

Answer the easiest questions first.

When you answer a question, be sure you are filling in the correct answer row.

American Artists

Art is something that people have in common around the world. In the next few pages, you will read about two of America's most interesting artists.

GO

Directions: Read this story about Gutzon Borglum, the man who made one of the largest sculptures on earth. Then do numbers 1–4.

The Man Who Made Mt. Rushmore Famous

If you have never heard of Gutzon Borglum, you are not alone. Even though he was the sculptor responsible for the carvings on Mount Rushmore, many people don't know him by name.

Gutzon Borglum was born in Idaho in 1867 to Danish parents. He became interested in art early in life. He spent some time studying art in Paris, then came back home to concentrate on sculpture. At the beginning of his career, Gutzon created many large sculptures, some that are quite famous. He also worked on the early stages of the carving of General Robert E. Lee at Stone Mountain, Virginia.

Gutzon was patriotic and outspoken. He lived during a time in American history that he called "the Colossal Age." This meant that big things were happening. For this reason, Gutzon Borglum became known as an artist who did things on a grand scale.

Borglum wanted to create a large monument to the four American Presidents who brought our country into the modern age. He located Mount Rushmore, a 5725-foot granite mountain in South Dakota, and began his sculptures in 1927. Working on one part at a time, Gutzon carved the faces of George Washington, Thomas Jefferson, Abraham Lincoln, and Theodore Roosevelt into the mountainside. In 1939, he finished Roosevelt, and continued to work on the details of the monument.

Gutzon Borglum died in 1941, but the work on Mount Rushmore was continued by his son, Lincoln. Fifty years later, in 1991, after all the details had been completed, Gutzon Borglum's monument in stone was honored in a final dedication ceremony. Today, it is one of the most visited national monuments.

GO

1 According to the passage, Gutzon Borglum did things on a *grand scale*. Doing something on a *grand scale* probably means

A making things that are fancy and overly decorated.

B making things that are very large and impressive.

C doing things very well and with great care.

D doing things that most people can't understand.

2 Based on your answer for number 1, which of the following works of art would you consider to be done on a grand scale?

F a painting of the members of a very large family

G a painting as tall as a house

H a drawing of the largest bridge in the world

J a life-size sculpture of a man

3 What did Gutzon Borglum do before he carved Mount Rushmore?

A He did some of the carving at Stone Mountain.

B He completed the sculptures at Stone Mountain.

C He made several other sculptures on mountains.

D He made carvings of several American Presidents.

4 Which of these statements about Mount Rushmore is true according to information in the article?

F It is the largest mountain in the country.

G It is the largest sculpture in the country.

H It is located in South Dakota.

J It is located in Virginia.

GO

Directions: For numbers 5 and 6, choose the sentence that best fills the blank in each paragraph.

5

> You might have heard of the Vietnam Veterans' Memorial in Washington, D. C., but have you heard of the Vietnam Women's Memorial? _____ The metal sculpture was officially dedicated on Veterans Day in 1993. It is located near the Vietnam Veterans' Memorial, in one of the most heavily visited areas of the capital city.

A   Many people visit the Vietnam monuments each year.

B   There is no admission fee to see this important monument.

C   It is a monument to the American women who served in Vietnam.

D   There are many other things to do and see in our nation's capital.

6

> The sculpture was designed by New Mexican artist Glenna Goodacre and funded by the Vietnam Women's Memorial Project. It shows three military women in various poses. _____ The monument reminds us that women played an important role in the Vietnam War.

F   One of the women is shown helping a wounded man.

G   Glenna Goodacre has created many other works of art.

H   Some of the women soldiers were from New Mexico.

J   Many soldiers lost their lives in the Vietnam War.

GO

Directions: Female artists were not often recognized in the nineteenth century. An exception to this rule was the American painter Mary Cassatt. Read about her life, then do numbers 7–14.

Mary Cassatt

Some people decide on a career early in life. That is what happened to Mary Cassatt, who dedicated herself to becoming an artist when she was very young. Mary Cassatt was born in Allegheny City, Pennsylvania, in 1844. Her father was a successful businessman of French origin, and his wealth allowed his family to travel around the world. As a child, Mary visited Paris, France, and saw paintings by famous artists. She knew right then what she wanted to do with her life.

Mary started small by studying at the Pennsylvania Academy of Fine Arts in Philadelphia. During this time, she continued to travel to foreign countries. In 1874, when Cassatt was thirty years old, she decided she was ready to leave home. She moved to Paris to work with other artists. She also spent long hours by herself, making copies of the works of great French painters.

After a short visit to the United States, Cassatt went back to Europe. This time, she traveled to Italy to study in an art academy and learn some different ways to paint. After her stay in Italy, she returned to her home in Paris.

At that time, one of the signs of a painter's success was to be accepted into the "Paris Salon," a large art show. Cassatt's work appeared in the show almost every year between 1872 and 1876. After such a triumph, she became a part of a group of painters called the Impressionists. One of the other famous members of this group, Edgar Degas, inspired her very much and became her lifelong friend.

The Impressionists started a new kind of painting; they painted things in a realistic way, the way they saw them. Cassatt used clear, bold colors for her work to make her paintings look lifelike. Her favorite subjects for paintings were women and children, who were shown doing normal, everyday things. For example, one of her well-known paintings shows a mother feeding her baby. Another one is of a little girl sitting in a blue chair.

GO

Cassatt's style and talent made her one of the most popular artists of her time. Her paintings are in museums all over the world. She spent the rest of her life in Paris, producing many beautiful pieces of art and enjoying great success. She died in 1926 after living her childhood dream of making a great name for herself as an artist.

7 **Here are pictures of events in the same order in which they happened in Mary Cassatt's life.**

Pennsylvania Academy

Paris

Italy

What should the missing picture show?

A

B

C

D

GO

8   Based on what you read in the passage, which word pair best fits
in this sentence?

Mary Cassatt's _____ led to her _____.

F   success . . . determination

G   travels . . . talent

H   dedication . . . success

J   wealth . . . dedication

---

9   Which of these best describes what happens in the passage?

A   A young girl grows up to be a famous painter.

B   A famous artist inspires a young girl to move to Paris.

C   A French artist paints many pictures about children.

D   A man takes his family to live in Paris.

---

10   The author says that Mary Cassatt "started small" to show that the young girl

F   wanted to become a great painter in under one year.

G   knew she had to learn the basics before leaving home.

H   didn't ever want to become a famous artist.

J   wanted to begin by doing only miniature paintings.

GO

11 **Choose the sentence that best fills the blank in the paragraph.**

> In the nineteenth century, Paris was a busy, important city. Because it was the capital of France, it was a business and political center. _____. Many well-known painters lived and worked there.

A Because of smog, it was not a very good place to live.

B It was difficult for young people to find work.

C Paris was also an important center of art.

D For example, it was the largest city in the country.

12 **If a student wanted to learn more about Mary Cassatt and other women painters, which of these books would be most helpful?**

F *Painting 1-2-3*

G *The Role of Women in American History*

H *Painting in the French Tradition*

J *Prominent Female Artists*

13 **What is the meaning of the word *signs* as it is used in the sentence below?**

At that time, one of the signs of a painter's success was to be accepted into the "Paris Salon," a large art show.

A roadside markers

B indications of a fact

C informative posters

D symbols used in horoscopes

14 **Which sentence best combines these two sentences into one?**

Mary left Pennsylvania.

Mary moved to Paris.

F Mary left Pennsylvania and moved to Paris.

G Mary left Pennsylvania and then Mary moved to Paris.

H Mary moved to Paris as she was leaving Pennsylvania.

J Mary, moving to Paris, left Pennsylvania.

GO

Directions: This paragraph tells what it was like to travel overseas in Mary Cassatt's time. There are some mistakes that need correcting.

[1] Until the 1950s, traveling from the United States to Europe was not as easy as getting on an airplane. [2] Travelers had to make a reservation in advance to have a small room on a ship. [3] Once on board, it took weeks to go from New York to a port city in Europe. [4] Then to a city like Paris it tooked days to go by train. [5] It was also expensive, so traveling around the world wasn't for everyone.

15 **What is the best way to write Sentence 4?**

A Then taking days to go by train to a city like Paris.

B Then it took days to go by train to a city like Paris.

C Then to go by train to a city like Paris taking days.

D Best as it is

16 **Choose the best way to write Sentence 2.**

F Travelers has to make a reservation in advance to have a small room on a ship.

G Travelers having to make a reservation in advance to have a small room on a ship.

H Travelers have to make a reservation in advance for having a small room on a ship.

J Best as it is

STOP

Lesson 2   Reading Fiction

Collecting

Millions of people around the world share the same hobby, collecting. Some collections are extremely unusual, such as paper clips, light bulbs, and even barbed wire. The next story you will read is about a special collection.

SAMPLE C   Scoop loved his nickname. His friends had called him that ever since he joined the school newspaper. He still hadn't written a big story, but he hoped to get a "scoop" soon.

In this story, the word *scoop* probably means

A a school paper.   **B** an assignment.   **C** a big story.   **D** a student.

 Skip difficult items and come back to them after you have tried the other items.

The right answer might not be given directly in the story. You may have to "read between the lines."

Directions: Read this story about a birthday party, then do numbers 17–21.

The Special Gift

"Happy Birthday to you!" everyone sang as T.J. prepared to blow out the eleven candles on his cake.

"Not so fast, mister," his mother said. "I think you have one more present coming."

"Really? What is it?" T.J. asked.

His father rose from his seat and walked around to T.J.'s chair. "Son, I have been waiting for this day to give you a very special gift. My father gave it to me when I was about your age, and it has been one of my most valued possessions. Now I want to give it to you." He then placed a dusty shoe box tied with string in front of T.J.

GO

"This is my stamp collection, son," his father began. "Your grandfather and I worked on it together, and now I want you to have it. I'll teach you about the different stamps and show you how to preserve them. We can go to the post office tomorrow after school, and you can pick out one of the new stamp sets to add to your collection."

T.J. tried to be excited about his gift, but he didn't understand what was so great about a box of old stamps. "Thanks, dad," he said, with a forced smile.

Then he noticed that Felicia had taken the box and was looking in each of the envelopes inside. "Look at this one!" she exclaimed. "It's from the year I was born. Hey, T.J., that's the year you were born, too!"

"That's right," said T.J.'s grandfather. "There are stamps from every year of the century, and extra ones from the year you were born. We were kind of celebrating," he added with a wink.

T.J. began to understand why the box was so important to his father and grandfather. He moved over by Felicia so that he could see the stamps better. Twenty minutes later, he didn't even notice that his ice cream had melted all over his birthday cake.

17 **When Felicia finds the stamps from the year she and T.J. were born, T.J. begins to understand that**

A he and Felicia are about the same age.

B some of the stamps are older than he is.

C the stamps are very meaningful.

D he was born after the collection was started.

18 **T.J. didn't notice that his ice cream was melting because**

F he was no longer very hungry.

G he was interested in the stamps.

H he didn't like chocolate ice cream.

J he had already left the table.

19 **In the sentence "I'll teach you about the different stamps and show you how to preserve them," the word** *preserve* **probably means**

A to keep in good condition.

B to give away as a gift.

C to show off to your friends.

D to sell to make money.

GO

20 If you wanted to learn more about stamp collecting, which of these would be your best source of information?

F a dictionary

H a current newspaper

G an atlas of the world

J an encyclopedia

21 Choose the picture that looks most like the box T.J.'s father gave him.

A   **B**   **C**   **D**

Directions: For his students, Mr. Heward prepared this outline about collecting stamps. Use the outline to do numbers 22 and 23.

THE BASICS OF STAMP COLLECTING

I   History of stamps in the United States
   A   Short introduction to stamps
   B   The first American stamps

II _____
   A   The first stamp collectors
   B   How stamp collecting got so popular
   C   The Post Office's role in stamp collecting

III How to begin your collection
   A   _____
   B   How to know the value of stamps
   C   Where to go for supplies

IV How to preserve your collection
   A   How to handle fragile stamps
   B   Guidelines for proper storage

22 Line II is blank. Which of these best fits there?

F The cost of collecting stamps

G Where to store your collection

H The history of stamp collecting

J Removing stamps from envelopes

23 Line III-A is blank. Which of these best fits there?

A Buying and trading postage stamps

B Stamps used during World War II

C The biggest stamp collection in the world

D Other kinds of collections you can start

STOP

Lesson 3 Review

SAMPLE D **Which of the following is an example of a fact?**

A Almost everybody in Colorado skis.

C The best school in Denver is Jennings Elementary.

B Denver is the capital of Colorado.

D The weather in Colorado is better than in Nebraska.

World Traveler and Sixth Grade Student

Directions: Read this interview of Vanessa Tomesky from a school paper. Then do numbers 24–28.

Vanessa Tomesky's parents are in the United States Air Force. Her family has lived in several places around the world, and she has some interesting stories to tell.

Reporter: *How old were you when you first moved to a foreign country?*

Vanessa Tomesky: I don't remember very much about moving. My parents were transferred to the Aviano Air Base in the northern part of Italy when I was four years old.

Reporter: *Do you remember anything about living there?*

Vanessa Tomesky: I lived there until I was eight years old, so I remember some things. It got very cold in the winter and very hot in the summer. The old women in the town were very nice to me, and I had a lot of friends.

I really liked my elementary school on the base. All of the American students took Italian classes. The teacher was friendly, and she showed us how to cook Italian food.

Reporter: *Were you sad when you had to leave?*

Vanessa Tomesky: I was starting to like Italy a lot when we left. The night Mom told me we were moving to Ramstein, in Germany, I cried myself to sleep!

GO

Reporter: *Was Germany very different from Italy?*

Vanessa Tomesky: Yes and no. We still lived on a military base with other American families, but this base was much bigger. I got lost a few times before I learned my way around. School was different because we had to learn German. I felt like I had learned Italian for nothing!

Luckily, I became friends with another new student, named Alex, who was living in England before he moved to Ramstein. Alex and I still write letters to each other.

My family lived in Germany for only two years, and I have been back in the United States since last summer. It was fun to travel, but I'm happy to be back. I can finally understand everything my teacher says!

Reporter: *What was the best thing about living in a foreign country?*

Vanessa Tomesky: The best part was getting to meet people from all over. I learned that kids are about the same everywhere.

Reporter: *What was the worst part?*

Vanessa Tomesky: There were two things I didn't like. First, it was always hard to leave my friends when we moved. Second, they don't celebrate my favorite holiday, Halloween, in other countries. I didn't get to go trick-or-treating for a long time!

---

24 **Which of these statements by Vanessa Tomesky best shows that she likes to make new friends?**

   A We still lived on a military base with other American families, but this base was much bigger.

   B I really liked my elementary school on the base.

   C Alex and I still write letters to each other.

   D The best part was getting to meet people from all over.

25 **For Vanessa, moving to a new school meant**

   F a new set of school rules.

   G dressing differently.

   H eating different kinds of food.

   J learning a new language.

GO

26 **Which of the following statements is an example of an opinion?**

A Vanessa learned to speak some Italian and some German during her travels.

B The best thing about being home was being able to celebrate Halloween.

C The German base was much bigger than the one in Italy had been.

D Vanessa doesn't remember very much about moving to Italy.

27 **Vanessa's Italian teacher taught the students how to**

do special dances.
F

decorate the classroom with artwork.
G

prepare food.
H

draw and paint.
J

28 **The interview is mostly about**

A Vanessa's experiences learning foreign languages.

B Vanessa's experiences living in foreign countries.

C Vanessa's favorite things about being home again.

D Vanessa's family and how they get along.

STOP

Language Arts

Lesson 1 Vocabulary

Directions: For Sample A and numbers 1 and 2, read the sentences. Choose the word that correctly completes both sentences.

Directions: For Sample B and numbers 3 and 4, choose the word that means the opposite of the underlined word.

SAMPLE A

Did someone _____ the cookies?
Leather is the _____ of an animal.

A eat   C skin

B hide   D bake

SAMPLE B

<u>remove</u> books

A purchase   C borrow

B read   D leave

---

1 This _____ is for the dog.
The yard was full of _____.

A comb   C collar

B weeds   D brush

2 Try to _____ the nail carefully.
The workers went on _____.

F strike   H leave

G hit   J place

3 <u>proper</u> behavior

A acceptable   C amusing

B incorrect   D confusing

4 <u>include</u> both

F invite   H notify

G exclude   J replace

Stay with your first answer. Change it only if you are sure another one is better.

GO

Directions: For numbers 5 and 6, read the sentences with the missing word and the question about that word. Choose the word that best answers the question.

5 The scientist _____ the samples. Which word means the scientist moved the samples apart?

A requested   C joined

B separated   D classified

6 Pam began to _____ about the vote. Which word means Pam became uncertain about the vote?

F waver   H retain

G argue   J stabilize

Directions: For numbers 7 and 8, choose the word that means the same, or about the same, as the underlined word.

7 surprising <u>outcome</u>

A announcement

B relationship

C question

D result

8 <u>possessed</u> information

F questioned

G discovered

H had

J lost

Directions: For numbers 9 and 10, read the paragraph. For each numbered blank, there is a list of words with the same number. Choose the word from each list that best completes the meaning of the paragraph.

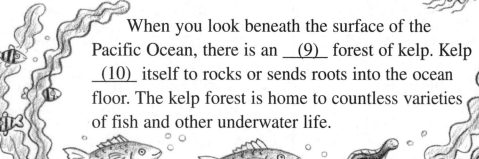

When you look beneath the surface of the Pacific Ocean, there is an __(9)__ forest of kelp. Kelp __(10)__ itself to rocks or sends roots into the ocean floor. The kelp forest is home to countless varieties of fish and other underwater life.

9 A avid   C enormous

B incidental   D aggressive

10 F releases   H encounters

G avoids   J anchors

STOP

Lesson 2 Language Mechanics

Directions: Look at the underlined parts of the following sentences. Choose the answer that shows the best capitalization and punctuation for that part.

SAMPLE C

Yoshi spent a week at a sports <u>camp, next</u> year he hopes to go for two weeks.

  A camp next

  B camp. Next

  C camp. next

  D Correct as it is

Directions: Choose the sentence that is written correctly and shows the correct capitalization and punctuation.

SAMPLE D

  A The boy sitting next to carmen was late.

  B Robin now lives on first Street.

  C Is Mrs. Syles coming over today.

  D Julio and Thea want to be in a play.

Directions: For numbers 11–14, look at the underlined part of the sentence. Choose the answer that shows the best capitalization and punctuation for that part.

11 His family is from <u>Austin, the</u> capital of the state of Texas.

  A Austin. the   **C** Austin the

  B Austin. The   **D** Correct as it is

12 My bird <u>wasnt</u> in his cage.

  F wasnt'   **H** wasn't

  G was'nt   **J** Correct as it is

13 Grandma will sit next to <u>me, and,</u> Grandpa will sit by you.

  A me And   **C** me and,

  B me, and   **D** Correct as it is

14 "I will be back in about twenty <u>minutes, said</u> Juliana.

  F minutes said   **H** minutes," said

  G minutes?" said   **J** Correct as it is

Skim the whole item. Then look at it again, keeping in mind you are looking for correct capitalization and punctuation.

Remember, "Correct as it is" should not be chosen too often.

GO

Directions: For numbers 15 and 16, choose the answer that is written correctly and shows the correct capitalization and punctuation.

15 **A** Have you ever made homemade bread?

B Do we have any bread for making sandwiches.

C Does carlos like white or wheat bread.

D Is that dark bread good with vegetable soup,

16 **F** "Please bring in the newspaper, said Uncle Monty.

G Alifah asked, "How much does the newspaper cost?"

H My newspaper route sure keeps me busy" I said.

J Mr. Walters said, "I used to be a newspaper reporter?"

Directions: For numbers 17–20, read the letter and the underlined parts. Choose the answer that shows the best capitalization and punctuation for each part.

November 16, 2001

(17)   Dear Mohammed,

(18)   I wish you could come and visit me, there are so many fun things to do here in the city. I have school

(19)   vacation next month; and it would be great if you could come and stay for a while.

(20)   Your Friend,

Lisanne

17 **A** dear Mohammed

B dear Mohammed,

C Dear Mohammed

D Correct as it is

18 **F** me there   **H** me? There

G me. There   **J** Correct as it is

19 **A** month and   **C** month, and

B month And   **D** Correct as it is

20 **F** Your friend,   **H** Your friend

G Your Friend   **J** Correct as it is

STOP

Lesson 3 Spelling

Directions: For Sample E and numbers 21–23, choose the word that is spelled correctly and best completes the sentence.

Directions: For Sample F and numbers 24 and 25, read each phrase. Find the underlined word that is *not* spelled correctly. If all the underlined words are spelled correctly, mark "All correct."

SAMPLE E The _____ will park the cars.

A attendant

B attendent

C atendent

D atendant

SAMPLE F

A restrict cars

B make a fortune

C missile landing

D discuss school

E All correct

21 We _____ what Mickey told us.

A beleived   C believded

B believed   D beliefed

22 The science _____ is open after school.

F labratory   H laboratry

G labaratory   J laboratory

23 The horse walked _____ the barn.

A towerd   C toward

B tward   D taword

24 A art museum

B unsold house

C diamond shaped

D wonderful spectacel

E All correct

25 F broken mirrorr

G small pieces

H lean meat

J outrageous clothes

K All correct

Don't spend too much time looking at the words. Pretty soon, they all begin to look like they are spelled wrong.

STOP

Lesson 4 Writing

Directions: Read the short fiction story.

The space taxi engine hummed in the background. David's teeth chattered. Little wells of moisture sprang up across his palms. *I can't fly,* he thought. *Mars is just around the corner, but it's too far for me.* David knew that his uncle was waiting for him, waiting for help with the space farm. At first, it didn't matter. In his mind, David saw himself hopping out of his taxi seat and bolting toward the door. But then he thought of his uncle's space fields. David knew that if he didn't help, the crops wouldn't be ready in the Mars 3 season. He took a deep breath and settled back for the flight. He couldn't wait to see the look on his uncle's face when he stepped off the taxi.

Directions: Now think about a fiction story that you would like to write. Write one or two sentences to answer each question below, and then use your answers to write a paragraph of your own.

Think about the main character. Who is it? What is he or she like?

_____

_____

What is the setting of the story? _____

_____

What kind of problem will the main character have? How will the character solve the problem? _____

_____

_____

Write your own short story on the lines below. _____

_____

_____

_____

GO

Directions: Read the paragraph below that compares two sports.

     I like both basketball and soccer. These sports are alike in some ways and different in others. Both are fast and challenging. I feel the same thrill when I move the ball across the soccer field as I do when I dribble down the basketball court. Unlike the outdoor soccer field, however, an indoor basketball court can be air-conditioned. It would be hard to decide between these two sports. Luckily, I can play them both.

Directions: Now think of two other things to compare and contrast, such as movies, musicians, or books. Use your ideas to write a paragraph. As you write, use words such as *same, like, different, unlike, but,* and *however.*

_____

_____

_____

_____

_____

_____

_____

_____

_____

_____

_____

_____

_____

STOP

Lesson 5 Review

Directions: For Sample G and number 26, choose the word that correctly completes both sentences.

> **SAMPLE G** How far can you _____ down the hill?
> The _____ of Oregon is beautiful.
>
> **A** coast   **C** ride
>
> **B** mountains   **D** forest

26 I had to _____ in line for tickets.
The fruit _____ will open at nine o'clock.

   A wait   **C** stand

   B store   **D** stay

Directions: For number 27, read the sentence with the missing word and the question about that word. Choose the word that best answers the question.

27 The sailors _____ their water supply.
Which word means the sailors refilled their water supply?

   F detected   **H** participated

   G allocated   **J** replenished

Directions: Find the underlined word that is *not* spelled correctly. If all the underlined words are spelled correctly, mark "All correct."

> **SAMPLE H**
> **A** powerful microscope
>
> **B** frowned at him
>
> **C** new computer
>
> **D** impossible problem
>
> **E** All correct

Directions: For number 28, choose the word that means the opposite of the underlined word.

28 willing to leave

   A able   **C** reluctant

   B eager   **D** allowed

Directions: For numbers 29 and 30, choose the word that means the same, or about the same, as the underlined word.

29 frank answer

   F short   **H** long

   G honest   **J** complicated

30 important data

   A computer   **C** information

   B meeting   **D** company

GO

Directions: For numbers 31 and 32, choose the answer that is written correctly and shows the correct capitalization and punctuation.

31 **F** You will have to look for that word in the *dictionary*.

G *The Velveteen Rabbit* was the best book I read last year.

H Have you ever read *The secret garden*?

J We have a one-year subscription to *newsweek* magazine.

32 **A** Camping in the snow is fun although, it can be dangerous.

B We wanted to go camping but, it rained.

C You may camp here, but, beware of poison oak.

D I like camping, but I don't like to hike.

Directions: For numbers 33–36, read the paragraph and the underlined parts. Choose the answer that shows the best capitalization and punctuation for each part.

On Saturdays, Petra and her dad ride their bikes to
(33) Grantville city park. They ride around the pond, then park their
(34) bikes and sit by the water. They count the ducks swans and frogs
(35) they see, and the one who counts the highest gets to lead the
(36) way home. As they ride past the water, Petra yells See you
       next Saturday!" to the animals in the pond.

33 **F** Grantville city Park.

G grantville city park

H Grantville City Park.

J Correct as it is

35 **F** see And

G see and,

H see, and,

J Correct as it is

34 **A** ducks, swans, and frogs

B ducks swans and, frogs

C ducks, swans and, frogs

D Correct as it is

36 **A** yells, See

B yells, "See

C yells see

D Correct as it is

GO

Directions: For numbers 37–40, choose the word that is spelled correctly and best completes the sentence.

37 It's best to follow your _____.

    F conscence

    G consience

    H conscience

    J consciense

38 We played with a _____ yesterday.

    A transister

    B transtistor

    C transisdor

    D transistor

39 Climbing the mountain was _____.

    F dangerus   **H** dangerous

    G dangeros   **J** dagerous

40 The judges were _____.

    A imparshall   **C** imparchel

    B imparcial   **D** impartial

Directions: For numbers 41–43, read each phrase. Find the underlined word that is *not* spelled correctly. If all the underlined words are spelled correctly, mark "All correct."

41 **F** <u>college</u> student

    G <u>tracing</u> paper

    H <u>calculate</u> answers

    J <u>succesful</u> business

    K All correct

42 **A** receive <u>justise</u>

    B <u>simplest</u> problem

    C wooden <u>fencing</u>

    D ancient <u>temple</u>

    E All correct

43 **F** positive <u>influence</u>

    G <u>security</u> system

    H baking <u>ingrediants</u>

    J granted <u>permission</u>

    K All correct

STOP

Directions: Read the book review.

I've just finished reading <u>A Wrinkle in Time</u> by Madeline L'Engle. This is one of the best books I've read all year. The events are unexpected. The characters are interesting, and the language is fresh and exciting. I highly recommend that you read this book.

Directions: Now think about a book you really enjoyed and why you think others would enjoy it. Use your ideas to write a book review of your own.

_____

_____

_____

_____

_____

_____

_____

_____

_____

_____

_____

_____

_____

_____

_____

_____

STOP

Lesson 1 Computation

SAMPLE A

$5.806 + 1.95 =$

A 3.856
B 7.711
C 7.756
D 8.756
E None of these

SAMPLE B

$21 \times 23 =$

F 44
G 463
H 2123
J 484
K None of these

 **TIPS**

Set the problem up correctly on scratch paper and work carefully.

Estimate the size of your answer. This will help you eliminate choices that are too large or too small.

1

$1.20
$0.80
$4.90

A $6.80
B $7.00
C $7.90
D $6.90
E None of these

3

$3.05 \times 500 =$

A $1525.00
B $1515.00
C $1535.00
D $1425.00
E None of these

2

$7\frac{3}{4} - 1\frac{1}{6} =$

F $6\frac{7}{12}$
G 6
H $6\frac{1}{2}$
J $7\frac{1}{2}$
K None of these

4

$32\overline{)5118}$

F 158
G 159 R30
H 159 R8
J 159 R28
K None of these

STOP

Lesson 2   Mathematics Skills

SAMPLE C   The shape being drawn in Graph 2 will be congruent to the shape in Graph 1. What will be the coordinates for Point A in Graph 2?

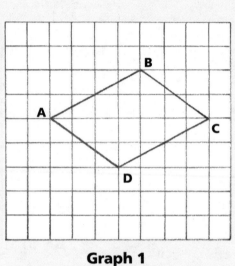

Graph 1

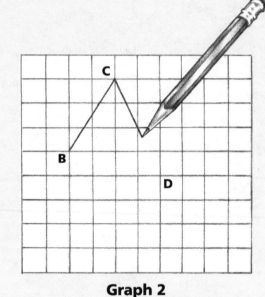

Graph 2

A   (3, 1)

B   (4, 2)

C   (4, 1)

D   (5, 2)

Think about what you are supposed to do before you start working.

Try the easiest items first.

Look for important words, numbers, and figures. They will help you find the answer.

GO

5 Nila rounded the number in the box to the nearest hundred thousand. And Elmo rerounded it to the nearest million.

> **2,689,123**

What was the difference between their answers?

A 300

C 30,000

B 3,000

D 300,000

6

> **(5 x 10,000,000) + (9 x 100,000) + (2 x 100) + 1**

Which of these numbers equals the expression shown above?

F 50,900,201

H 5,900,201

G 59,000,201

J 50,090,201

7 What rule is Brielle using to change "Now" numbers to "Later" numbers?

Now	7	18	30
Later	18	51	87

A add 5, then multiply by 2

B subtract 2, then multiply by 3

C add 1, then multiply by 3

D subtract 1, then multiply by 3

GO

Going to the Dogs

Directions: The graph shows the number of dogs registered with the American Kennel Club in 1994 and 1995. Study the graph. Then do numbers 8–10.

American Kennel Club Registration

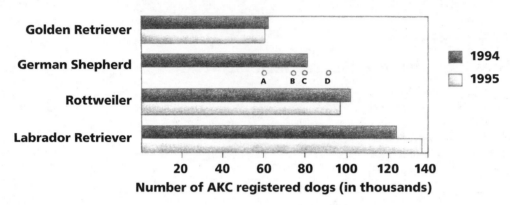

Number of AKC registered dogs (in thousands)

■ 1994
□ 1995

8 A premium dog food company is shooting a commercial with a dog in it. If the company wants to appeal to the largest number of pedigree dog owners, which breed of dog should they use?

F Labrador Retriever   **H** German Shepherd

G Rottweiler   **J** Golden Retriever

9 The number of American Kennel Club registered Rottweilers in 1995 was

A less than 90,000.

B between 90,000 and 100,000.

C between 100,000 and 110,000.

D more than 110,000.

10 The number of registered German Shepherds in 1995 was 78,088. Look at points A, B, C, and D on the graph. Which point indicates where a bar should be drawn to complete the graph?

F Point A   **H** Point C

G Point B   **J** Point D

GO

On the Boardwalk

Directions: Wanda and her family enjoy walking along the Boardwalk. Do numbers 11–16 about the Boardwalk.

11

Ringo runs the ring toss booth on the Boardwalk. Here is Ringo.

Which of these is Ringo?

A　　**B**　　**C**　　**D**

12 **About how much will the popcorn on the scale cost?**

F $0.80

G $2.50

H $3.25

J $4.95

13 **Each member of Wanda's family had one hamburger for lunch. Each hamburger costs $4.95. What else do you need to know to find out how much the family spent on lunch?**

A which family member paid for lunch

B how many people are in the family

C the price of hot dogs

D how much money Wanda's father had in his wallet

GO

14 These signs are all on the Boardwalk. Which sign has no right angles?

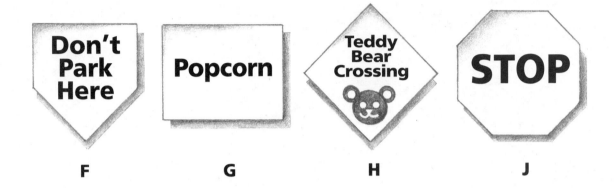

F   G   H   J

15 The guide book for the Boardwalk has a star that extends from the front cover to the back cover. How many points are on the star when the book is open?

A 5

B 6

C 7

D 8

16 The amusements are located on a pier off the Boardwalk. Which road runs parallel to the Boardwalk?

F Steeplechase Avenue

G Ferris Wheel Drive

H Roller Coaster Way

J Merry-Go-Round Street

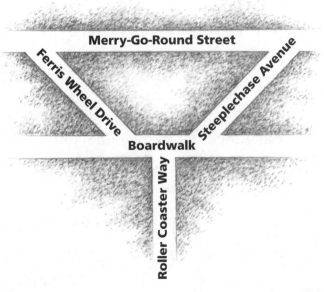

STOP

Lesson 3 **Review**

SAMPLE D 80% of 45 =

    A 35   **D** 36

    B 48   **E** None of these

    C 38

17
$$\begin{array}{r} 25 \\ 376 \\ 80 \\ + 8241 \\ \hline \end{array}$$

  A 8622

  B 722

  C 8720

  D 8721

  E None of these

18 $8\frac{2}{3} - 5\frac{1}{6}$

  F $5\frac{1}{3}$

  G $3\frac{1}{2}$

  H $1\frac{1}{3}$

  J $\frac{1}{8}$

  K None of these

19
$$\begin{array}{r} 6.548 \\ - 3.259 \\ \hline \end{array}$$

  A 3.289   **D** 3.299

  B 3.311   **E** None of these

  C 3.399

20
$$\begin{array}{r} 135 \\ \times\ 48 \\ \hline \end{array}$$

  F 6280   **J** 6480

  G 6440   **K** None of these

  H 5080

21
$$\begin{array}{r} 4.5 \\ \times\ .27 \\ \hline \end{array}$$

  A 12.15   **D** .1215

  B 1.215   **E** None of these

  C 121.5

GO

SAMPLE E **Which pair of curved lines is probably congruent?**

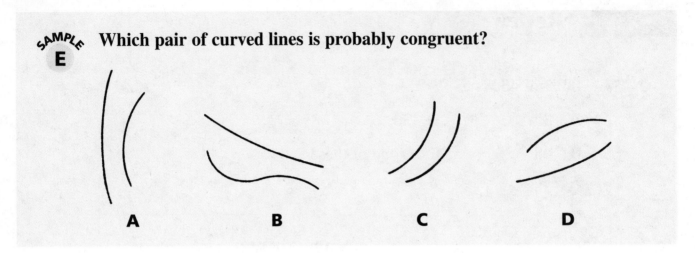

A   B   C   D

Perimeters, Please

Directions: The table shows the perimeters of squares with given side lengths. Study the table. Then do numbers 22 and 23.

Length of Side of Square	Perimeter of Square
1	4
2	8
3	12
4	16
5	20

22 **What is the perimeter of a square with sides of length 2.5?**

A 5

B 7.5

C 10

D 12.5

23 **What is the perimeter of the rectangle?**

F 2 inches

G $3\frac{1}{2}$ inches

H $4\frac{1}{2}$ inches

J 6 inches

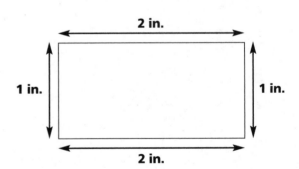

GO

24 Which of these graphs best shows how the perimeter of a square is related to the length of a side of the square?

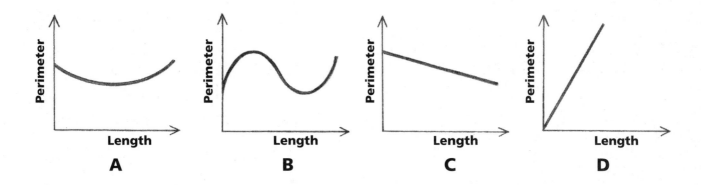

A

B

C

D

25 Nako is using nickels to measure the area of a dollar bill. About how many nickels will it take to cover the dollar bill?

F   about 50

G   about 21

H   about 18

J   about 10

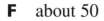

26 Sally and Susie together have more money in their piggy banks than Tom has in his. If Tom has $ 5.00 and Susie has $17.00, then Sally must have

A   less than $17.00.

B   exactly $18.00.

C   between $17.00 and $18.00.

D   more than $18.00.

GO

27 How many more glass balls are needed to fill the box to the top?

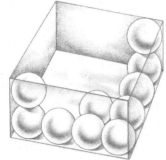

- **F** 20
- **G** 22
- **H** 24
- **J** 26

28 Lizette makes cubes from blocks to display kitchen gadgets and cookware in her store as shown below.

How many blocks will she use to make Display 6?

- **A** 36
- **B** 64
- **C** 125
- **D** 216

Display 1   Display 2   Display 3

29 Which of these numbers goes in the box to make the number sentence true?

□ < 50.05

- **F** 55.55
- **H** 50.005
- **G** 50.50
- **J** 55.05

30 What is the average of 12, 7, and 8?

- **A** 7
- **C** 9
- **B** 8
- **D** 27

31 If C and D represent whole numbers, what symbol goes in the box to make this statement true?

If C × D = 12, then 12 □ C = D.

- **F** +
- **G** −
- **H** ×
- **J** ÷

32 What is the rule for this number sequence? 5, 11, 29, 83, 245, . . .

- **A** multiply by 3, then add 5
- **B** multiply by 2, then add 1
- **C** multiply by 2, then add 7
- **D** multiply by 3, then subtract 4

33 The number 8 is _____ times larger than the number 0.0008.

- **F** 10
- **H** 1,000
- **G** 100
- **J** 10,000

STOP

Social Studies

Lesson 1

Directions: Study the time line that shows important events in ancient Egypt, and then do numbers 1–4.

| 8000 B.C. People come to the Nile River as they search for food. | 2050 B.C. The Middle Kingdom is established, granting greater rights to people. | 1570 B.C. The New Kingdom is established. Queen Hatshepsut begins her reign. |

| 3100 B.C. Earliest known hieroglyphics, pictograms, are created. | 331 B.C. Alexander the Great leads his soldiers to conquer Egypt. |

1 What event happened *earliest*?

A Pictographs were created.

B Queen Hatshepsut ruled.

C Alexander the Great conquered Egypt.

D The Middle Kingdom was established.

2 Which event happened *after* Queen Hatshepsut's reign?

F the beginning of hieroglyphics

G Alexander the Great's victory

H people beginning to gather at the Nile to search for food

J establishment of the Middle Kingdom

3 How many years after the beginning of Queen Hatshepsut's reign did Alexander the Great conquer Europe?

A 1,901 years   **C** 1,801 years

B 1,149 years   **D** 1,239 years

4 When were the earliest known hieroglyphics created?

F during Queen Hatshepsut's reign

G after the Middle Kingdom was established

H before Alexander the Great began his rule

J while people first came to the Nile River

GO

Directions: For Numbers 5–10, study the picture and then identify each landform.

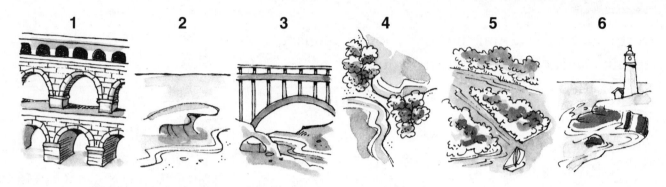

1   2   3   4   5   6

5   **Which land feature is labeled 1 in the picture above?**

   A isthmus   **C** ocean

   B bridge   **D** aqueduct

6   **Which land feature is labeled 2 in the picture above?**

   F ocean   **H** isthmus

   G delta   **J** aqueduct

7   **Which land feature is labeled 3 in the picture above?**

   A bridge   **C** aqueduct

   B cape   **D** isthmus

8   **Which land feature is labeled 4 in the picture above?**

   F cape   **H** isthmus

   G ocean   **J** bridge

9   **Which land feature is labeled 5 in the picture above?**

   A bridge   **C** delta

   B ocean   **D** isthmus

10 **Which land feature is labeled 6 in the picture above?**

   F aqueduct   **H** isthmus

   G cape   **J** bridge

STOP

Lesson 2   Review

11 **Which best describes a city-state of Mesopotamia?**

A a form of government in which leaders participated through countrywide elections

B a system of roads and bridges criss-crossing the region to provide transportation routes

C a river and system of housing that produced crops to feed the population

D a large town and surrounding countryside cooperating to stay safe

12 **Which statement about elections in the United States is *false*?**

F Members of the House of Representatives and the Senate are elected.

G Voters can cast ballots for local officials, as well as for national officials.

H Some judges are elected, and others are appointed.

J It is possible to have a Democratic president and a Republican vice president.

13 **Which best describes the electoral college in the United States?**

A a university where candidates learn how to conduct a campaign

B a system for electing the president and vice president

C a school where people can gain more information about voting

D a state-to-state connection of equipment that calculates votes

14 **How many senators from each state serve in the United States Congress?**

F 1

G 2

H 3

J The number of senators depends on the population of the state.

GO

Practice Test
Social Studies

Directions: Read the passage, and then do numbers 15–18.

Americans fought for the right to vote in the Revolutionary War; however, not all Americans had the right to vote before certain amendments to the United States Constitution were passed. Laws were enacted that allowed people to vote only if they had large amounts of money or owned their own property. A tax, called a *poll tax,* even required people to pay to vote! Women were not allowed to vote just because they were women. They were also expected to give all of their possessions and money to their husbands when they married. The Civil War ended slavery, but most African-Americans were still barred from voting because of their skin color. This changed with the Fifteenth, Nineteenth, and Twenty-fourth Amendments. The Fifteenth Amendment, passed in 1870, made it illegal to deny voting rights based on color or race. The Nineteenth Amendment gave women the right to vote in 1920. And poll taxes were prohibited by the Twenty-fourth Amendment, passed in 1964.

15 What is a poll tax?

   A a tax elected officials had to pay

   B funds paid to take polls

   C a fee paid by those running for office

   D money paid to gain voting rights

16 Which statement about voting rights is true?

   F Constitutional amendments limited voting rights.

   G The Nineteenth Amendment granted voting rights to African-Americans.

   H African-American men were allowed to vote before women were.

   J Constitutional amendments granted weak voting rights.

17 When did women gain the right to vote?

   A before the Civil War

   B in 1870

   C in 1964

   D in 1920

18 Which statement about voting rights is *false*?

   F A person must be at least eighteen years old.

   G Voters must own property.

   H Voters must be United States citizens.

   J Voters can be any race or color.

STOP

Science

Lesson 1

1 When two species live together in a way that is helpful to one or both species, it is called

   A heredity.   **C** symbiosis.

   B synergy.   **D** extinction.

2 Which animal is highest in the food chain?

   F insect   **H** snake

   G rat   **J** bear

3 Which animal would not be found in a pond ecosystem?

   A rabbit   **C** insect

   B fish   **D** frog

4 _____ occurs when people cut down large numbers of trees.

   F Replanting   **H** Dutch elm disease

   G Fertilization   **J** Deforestation

Directions: Read about one student's experiment on the greenhouse effect, and then do numbers 5 and 6.

Carol wanted to learn more about how the greenhouse effect affects particular ecosystems, so she created a mini ecosystem of her own. She got a large glass container and filled it halfway with soil. She put in leaves and twigs. Then she replanted some small plants from her garden. Finally she added a few earthworms, some beetles, and a butterfly cocoon.

5 What should Carol do to simulate the greenhouse effect?

   A Put the container in a cool, dark closet.

   B Expose the container to sunlight with little ventilation.

   C Water it frequently every day.

   D Add mice and rats.

6 If the plants die and the cocoon does not hatch, what could Carol conclude?

   F The greenhouse effect has no effect on her ecosystem.

   G She did a bad job of taking care of her plants and animals.

   H The greenhouse effect has a negative effect on her ecosystem.

   J The greenhouse effect has a positive effect on her ecosystem.

GO

7 **Most of the mass of an atom is in its**

   A electrons.

   B quarks.

   C charges.

   D nucleus.

8 **What kind of charge do electrons carry?**

   F positive

   G negative

   H electric

   J nuclear

9 **A molecule is formed when**

   A two or more atoms come together.

   B oxygen and hydrogen are burned.

   C electrons are stripped from an atom.

   D positive charges are combined with negative charges.

10 **What compound is formed when an acid and a base join?**

   F liquid nitrogen

   G a salt

   H glue

   J putty

11 **Which of the following would not be found in an animal cell?**

   A cell membrane

   B cell wall

   C cytoplasm

   D nucleus

12 **During asexual reproduction, chromosomes in a cell reproduce themselves in a process called**

   F cell division.

   G mitosis.

   H meiosis.

   J cytosis.

GO

Lesson 2 Review

13 **What part of a cell changes food into energy?**

    A cytoplasm

    B nucleus

    C mitochondria

    D vacuoles

14 **Which of the following statements is true for all cells?**

    F The nucleus of a cell is its "brain," or command center.

    G Cells are found only in plants and animals, not in humans.

    H Vacuoles live in the cell wall, where they store food and energy.

    J Animal cells contain chloroplasts.

Directions: Look at the cell diagram and then do numbers 15 and 16.

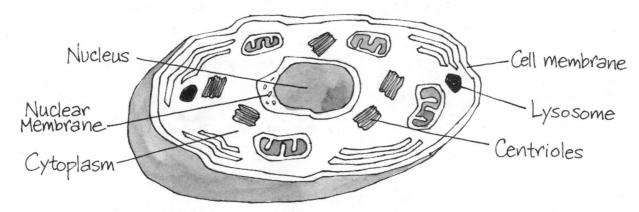

15 **What would be the best way to find out what kind of cell this is?**

    A Compare it to photos or drawings of other cells.

    B Check it closely every day.

    C Put the cell on a petri dish and watch it grow.

    D Suspend the cell in water.

16 **What tool would you use to examine this cell?**

    F hand lens

    G magnifying glass

    H microscope

    J telescope

GO

17 **How does light travel?**

   A in waves only

   B in particles only

   C in both waves and particles

   D in neither waves nor particles

18 **Emma sees a flash of lightning and then hears the thunder about 5 seconds later. Next, she sees another flash of lightning, and the thunder comes 2 seconds later. What can she conclude?**

   F The light is traveling faster than before.

   G The thunder is getting louder.

   H The lightning is closer than before.

   J The thunder is further away than before.

19 **What is the correct order of colors in the spectrum?**

   A red, yellow, orange, green, blue, violet, indigo

   B red, orange, yellow, green, blue, indigo, violet

   C red, green, orange, yellow, indigo, violet, blue

   D red, orange, yellow, green, blue, violet, indigo

20 **Objects are visible to us only when**

   F they are viewed in the correct atmosphere.

   G light is absorbed by them.

   H light is refracted off them.

   J light is reflected off them.

STOP

Final Test Answer Sheet

Fill in **only one** letter for each item. If you change an answer, make sure to erase your first mark completely.

Unit 1: Reading, pages 125–130

A (A) (B) (C) (D)   6 (F) (G) (H) (J)   12 (F) (G) (H) (J)   18 (F) (G) (H) (J)   24 (F) (G) (H) (J)

1 (A) (B) (C) (D)   7 (A) (B) (C) (D)   13 (A) (B) (C) (D)   19 (A) (B) (C) (D)   25 (F) (G) (H) (J)

2 (F) (G) (H) (J)   8 (F) (G) (H) (J)   14 (F) (G) (H) (J)   20 (A) (B) (C) (D)   26 (F) (G) (H) (J)

3 (A) (B) (C) (D)   9 (A) (B) (C) (D)   15 (A) (B) (C) (D)   21 (A) (B) (C) (D)

4 (F) (G) (H) (J)   10 (F) (G) (H) (J)   16 (F) (G) (H) (J)   22 (A) (B) (C) (D)

5 (A) (B) (C) (D)   11 (A) (B) (C) (D)   17 (A) (B) (C) (D)   23 (F) (G) (H) (J)

Unit 2: Language Arts, pages 131–139

A (A) (B) (C) (D)   10 (F) (G) (H) (J)   21 (A) (B) (C) (D)   32 (F) (G) (H) (J)

1 (A) (B) (C) (D)   11 (A) (B) (C) (D)   22 (F) (G) (H) (J)   33 (A) (B) (C) (D)

B (A) (B) (C) (D)   12 (F) (G) (H) (J)   23 (A) (B) (C) (D)   34 (F) (G) (H) (J)

2 (F) (G) (H) (J)   13 (A) (B) (C) (D)   24 (F) (G) (H) (J)   35 (A) (B) (C) (D)

3 (A) (B) (C) (D)   14 (F) (G) (H) (J)   25 (A) (B) (C) (D)   36 (F) (G) (H) (J)

4 (F) (G) (H) (J)   15 (A) (B) (C) (D) (E)   26 (F) (G) (H) (J)   37 (A) (B) (C) (D)

5 (A) (B) (C) (D)   16 (F) (G) (H) (J) (K)   27 (A) (B) (C) (D)   38 (F) (G) (H) (J)

6 (F) (G) (H) (J)   17 (A) (B) (C) (D) (E)   28 (F) (G) (H) (J)   39 (A) (B) (C) (D)

7 (A) (B) (C) (D)   18 (F) (G) (H) (J) (K)   29 (A) (B) (C) (D)   40 (F) (G) (H) (J)

8 (F) (G) (H) (J)   19 (A) (B) (C) (D)   30 (F) (G) (H) (J)   41 (A) (B) (C) (D)

9 (A) (B) (C) (D)   20 (F) (G) (H) (J)   31 (A) (B) (C) (D)

Final Test Answer Sheet

Unit 3: Mathematics, pages 140–148

A Ⓐ Ⓑ Ⓒ Ⓓ Ⓔ	**8** Ⓕ Ⓖ Ⓗ Ⓙ Ⓚ	**18** Ⓕ Ⓖ Ⓗ Ⓙ	**28** Ⓕ Ⓖ Ⓗ Ⓙ
B Ⓕ Ⓖ Ⓗ Ⓙ Ⓚ	**9** Ⓐ Ⓑ Ⓒ Ⓓ	**19** Ⓐ Ⓑ Ⓒ Ⓓ	**29** Ⓐ Ⓑ Ⓒ Ⓓ
1 Ⓐ Ⓑ Ⓒ Ⓓ Ⓔ	**10** Ⓕ Ⓖ Ⓗ Ⓙ	**20** Ⓕ Ⓖ Ⓗ Ⓙ	**30** Ⓕ Ⓖ Ⓗ Ⓙ
2 Ⓕ Ⓖ Ⓗ Ⓙ Ⓚ	**11** Ⓐ Ⓑ Ⓒ Ⓓ	**21** Ⓐ Ⓑ Ⓒ Ⓓ	**31** Ⓐ Ⓑ Ⓒ Ⓓ
3 Ⓐ Ⓑ Ⓒ Ⓓ Ⓔ	**12** Ⓕ Ⓖ Ⓗ Ⓙ	**22** Ⓕ Ⓖ Ⓗ Ⓙ	**32** Ⓕ Ⓖ Ⓗ Ⓙ
4 Ⓕ Ⓖ Ⓗ Ⓙ Ⓚ	**13** Ⓐ Ⓑ Ⓒ Ⓓ	**23** Ⓐ Ⓑ Ⓒ Ⓓ	**33** Ⓐ Ⓑ Ⓒ Ⓓ
5 Ⓐ Ⓑ Ⓒ Ⓓ Ⓔ	**14** Ⓕ Ⓖ Ⓗ Ⓙ	**24** Ⓕ Ⓖ Ⓗ Ⓙ	**34** Ⓕ Ⓖ Ⓗ Ⓙ
6 Ⓕ Ⓖ Ⓗ Ⓙ Ⓚ	**15** Ⓐ Ⓑ Ⓒ Ⓓ	**25** Ⓐ Ⓑ Ⓒ Ⓓ	**35** Ⓐ Ⓑ Ⓒ Ⓓ
C Ⓐ Ⓑ Ⓒ Ⓓ	**16** Ⓕ Ⓖ Ⓗ Ⓙ	**26** Ⓕ Ⓖ Ⓗ Ⓙ	
7 Ⓐ Ⓑ Ⓒ Ⓓ	**17** Ⓐ Ⓑ Ⓒ Ⓓ	**27** Ⓐ Ⓑ Ⓒ Ⓓ	

Unit 4: Social Studies, pages 149–150

1 Ⓐ Ⓑ Ⓒ Ⓓ	**3** Ⓐ Ⓑ Ⓒ Ⓓ	**5** Ⓐ Ⓑ Ⓒ Ⓓ	**7** Ⓐ Ⓑ Ⓒ Ⓓ	**9** Ⓐ Ⓑ Ⓒ Ⓓ
2 Ⓕ Ⓖ Ⓗ Ⓙ	**4** Ⓕ Ⓖ Ⓗ Ⓙ	**6** Ⓕ Ⓖ Ⓗ Ⓙ	**8** Ⓕ Ⓖ Ⓗ Ⓙ	**10** Ⓕ Ⓖ Ⓗ Ⓙ

Unit 5: Science, pages 151–152

1 Ⓐ Ⓑ Ⓒ Ⓓ	**3** Ⓐ Ⓑ Ⓒ Ⓓ	**5** Ⓐ Ⓑ Ⓒ Ⓓ	**7** Ⓐ Ⓑ Ⓒ Ⓓ
2 Ⓕ Ⓖ Ⓗ Ⓙ	**4** Ⓕ Ⓖ Ⓗ Ⓙ	**6** Ⓕ Ⓖ Ⓗ Ⓙ	

Pages 125–130
Time Limit:
approx. 35 minutes

Reading

Final Test
Reading   UNIT 1

SAMPLE A

[1] Some animals are collectors. [2] The pack rat, for example, collects all sorts of objects it finds in the desert. [3] It especially likes shiny things that people drop. [4] A pack rat's nest is often filled with hundreds of things it has collected.

Choose the best way to write Sentence 3.

A   Shiny things it especially likes that people drop.

B   People drop shiny things especially that it likes.

C   Liking shiny things, people drop them especially.

D   Best as it is

Directions: Penny wrote a story for the school paper about another kind of collection. For the first part of the report, choose the answer that best fills the blank in the paragraph.

Buttons, Buttons, Buttons

I have been collecting buttons since I was in the fourth grade. I don't collect the kind of buttons you find on your clothes, just the kind with pictures or sayings printed on them. _____.

Have a Nice Day

1   A   On the other hand, some of my buttons are from political campaigns.

B   For example, some of my buttons are from political campaigns.

C   However, some of my buttons are from political campaigns.

D   In other words, some of my buttons are from political campaigns.

GO

Directions: Now read the second part of the story. Some mistakes need correcting.

> ¹ Some of my buttons are worth money, but most are just valuable to me. ² I like to look at them because they remind me of people I know or things I have doing. ³ My favorite buttons are the ones with jokes or funny pictures. ⁴ One of these is pink and says "I'm not just another pretty face, you know!" ⁵ Others have cartoon characters or animals on them. ⁶ When I visit a zoo or amusement park, my mother lets me buy a button. ⁷ She gives me a button every year on my birthday, too. ⁸ More actually, it is because of my mom that my collection has grown.

2 **Choose the best way to write Sentence 2.**

F I like to look at them because they remind me of people I know or things I having done.

G I like to look at them because they remind me of people I know or things I have done.

H I like to look at them because they remind me of people I am knowing or things I am doing.

J Best as it is

3 **The best way to write Sentence 7 is:**

A Her gives me a button every year on my birthday, too.

B She gives me a button every year on me birthday, too.

C She gives my a button every year on my birthday, too.

D Best as it is

4 **The best way to write Sentence 8 is:**

F Actually, it is because of my mom that my collection has grown.

G Actual, it is because of my mom that my collection has grown.

H More actual, it is because of my mom that my collection has grown.

J Best as it is

GO

Directions: Now read the last part of the story.

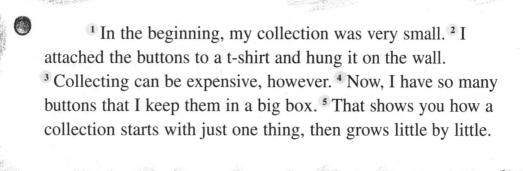

¹ In the beginning, my collection was very small. ² I attached the buttons to a t-shirt and hung it on the wall. ³ Collecting can be expensive, however. ⁴ Now, I have so many buttons that I keep them in a big box. ⁵ That shows you how a collection starts with just one thing, then grows little by little.

5 **Choose the sentence that is complete and is written correctly.**

A It can be fun to start a collection, start one today.

B Buttons can be displayed on a wall or stored in a box.

C Buttons are small and inexpensive and, easy to store.

D Every collection starts small and getting bigger.

6 **Which sentence does <u>not</u> belong in the paragraph?**

F Sentence 1

G Sentence 3

H Sentence 4

J Sentence 5

GO

Directions: Penny decided to take an inventory of her buttons by size and type. She then put the results in a chart. Use it to do numbers 7–9.

My Button Collection

Button type	Small	Medium	Large	Total
Political campaigns	3	9	2	14
Animals or zoos	2	8	5	15
Health or exercise	0	7	3	10
Jokes or funny sayings	3	8	0	11
School spirit	2	6	2	10
Other	1	2	5	8
Total	11	40	17	

7 **Penny has mostly**

A small buttons.   **C** large buttons.

B medium buttons.   **D** campaign buttons.

8 **How many of the buttons could be about the benefits of healthy eating?**

F 10   **H** 13

G 11   **J** 18

9 **Suppose you know the student who made this chart, and you give her a button as a gift. The button has a picture of an elephant and the words "Happy Birthday!" When she next fills in her chart, the button you gave her will go**

A in the category called "School spirit."

B in the category called "Other."

C in the "Jokes or funny sayings" category.

D in the "Animals or zoos" category.

GO

Directions: Read the passage. Then answer the questions.

Animal lovers throughout the world adore koalas. Yet these cuddly creatures' very existence is threatened! Greedy humans in koalas' Australian homeland are thoughtlessly destroying **eucalyptus** forests to make room for more homes and shopping malls. Koalas need a variety of eucalyptus species, or they will not eat. It is essential that the forests be protected if koalas are to survive. It would be tragic if the darling furry animals were sacrificed just to build a few shopping malls! To contribute to our **cause**, call **1-555-4koalas** today!

10 The most appropriate title for this passage would be

F "Urgent Message: Save the Koalas!"

G "Eucalyptus Forests."

H "Australian Wildlife Protection."

J "Koalas' Shrinking Habitat."

11 In this passage, the word *cause* means

A something that makes something else happen.

B a goal.

C the reason for a certain feeling or action.

D to make happen.

12 In which of the following would you be most likely to find this passage?

F personal narrative

G autobiography

H fiction book

J advertisement

13 A *eucalyptus* is a kind of

A home. **C** tree.

B animal. **D** insect.

14 What was the author's purpose for writing this passage?

F to provide information about koalas' habits

G to provide information about eucalyptus forests

H to raise money to protect koalas' habitat

J to help Australians build their economy

GO

Directions: Choose the best answer for each of the following.

15 <u>Complicated</u> is to <u>intricate</u> as <u>important</u> is to _____.

    A essential   **C** terrible

    B unimportant   **D** good

16 <u>Gram</u> is to <u>kilogram</u> as <u>milliliter</u> is to _____.

    F liter

    G kilometer

    H kilogram

    J milligram

17 <u>Hardware</u> is to <u>computer monitor</u> as <u>software</u> is to _____.

    A keyboard

    B computer

    C word processing program

    D download

18 <u>Playwright</u> is to <u>play</u> as <u>biographer</u> is to _____.

    F science fiction   **H** newspaper

    G autobiography   **J** life story

Directions: Match words with the *same* meanings.

19 **misfortune**   **A** hoist

20 **lift**   **B** least

21 **ridiculous**   **C** calamity

22 **minimum**   **D** absurd

Directions: Match words with the *opposite* meanings.

23 **identical**   **F** carelessly

24 **gingerly**   **G** dissimilar

25 **commence**   **H** conclude

26 **endanger**   **J** protect

STOP

0:35
Pages 131–137
Time Limit:
approx. 35 minutes

Language Arts

Final Test
Language Arts

UNIT **2**

Directions: For Sample A and number 1, read the sentences. Choose the word that correctly completes both sentences.

> **SAMPLE A** The _____ piece goes here.
> The first _____ of the tournament is over.
>
> **A** square   **C** round
>
> **B** part   **D** circular

Directions: Choose the word that is spelled correctly and best completes the sentence.

> **SAMPLE B** The _____ to read is important.
>
> **A** abilitie   **C** abality
>
> **B** abilty   **D** ability

1 This _____ will smooth the wood.
The _____ arrived at five o'clock.

A tool   **C** bus

B train   **D** plane

Directions: For number 2, choose the word that means the **opposite** of the underlined word.

2 <u>simple</u> room

F ornate

G empty

H full

J unusual

Directions: For numbers 3 and 4, read the paragraph. For each numbered blank, there is a list of words with the same number. Choose the word from each list that best completes the meaning of the paragraph.

Kate was ___(3)___ when she was chosen to represent her school in the "Brain Game." This annual event gave students in her state the chance to compete in a test of general knowledge. Kate was looking forward to the competition. The winner would be ___(4)___ the state's academic champion.

3 **A** disappointed   **C** bothered

B indifferent   **D** delighted

4 **F** declared   **H** justified

G invited   **J** deceived

GO

Directions: For numbers 5 and 6, choose the answer that is written correctly and shows the correct capitalization and punctuation.

5
 A Was your aunt born in San Francisco, California?

 B New orleans, Louisiana is where my cousins live.

 C Her stepfather grew up in Chicago Illinois?

 D Tucson, arizona is the home of my grandparents.

6
 F "Let's go on a picnic, suggested Josefina.

 G Marty asked, you forgot our picnic lunch?

 H "This picnic table is just right," said Mom.

 J "No ants allowed on my picnic blanket yelled Vivian.

Directions: For numbers 7–10, look at the underlined part of the paragraph. Choose the answer that shows the best capitalization and punctuation for that part.

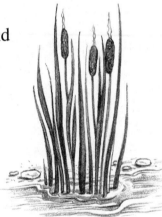

(7)   The state just bought <u>Hardy Lake</u>. It will be used for
(8) <u>swimming boating, and fishing.</u> A local newspaper will
(9) <u>sponsor. A picnic</u> area there. Our town will build a nature
(10) center near the <u>lake: and</u> students from Valley Elementary
School will serve as guides.

7
 A hardy lake.

 B Hardy lake.

 C Hardy Lake?

 D Correct as it is

8
 F swimming, boating, and fishing.

 G swimming boating and fishing.

 H swimming, boating, and, fishing.

 J Correct as it is

9
 A sponsor a picnic.

 B sponsor, a picnic.

 C sponsor a picnic

 D Correct as it is

10
 F Lake. And

 G lake, and

 H lake and,

 J Correct as it is

GO

Directions: For numbers 11–14, choose the word that is spelled correctly and best completes the sentence.

11 **The boat _____ toward shore.**

   A driffed

   B drifted

   C drifded

   D drifteded

12 **My socks are in the _____.**

   F bureaou

   G bureow

   H buroaw

   J bureau

13 **Winter follows _____ .**

   A autunm   **C** autum

   B autume   **D** autumn

14 **He _____ the math facts.**

   F memorised   **H** memerized

   G memorized   **J** memmorized

Directions: For numbers 15–18, read each phrase. Find the underlined word that is *not* spelled correctly. If all the underlined words are spelled correctly, mark "All correct."

15 **A** <u>justice</u> for all

   B a new <u>category</u>

   C the secret <u>ingredient</u>

   D the tricky <u>magician</u>

   E All correct

16 **F** don't be <u>contrarie</u>

   G the <u>concealed</u> door

   H our <u>debating</u> club

   J the science <u>exposition</u>

   K All correct

17 **A** <u>weather</u> vane

   B little <u>difference</u>

   C <u>seiling</u> fan

   D <u>successful</u> plan

   E All correct

18 **F** <u>transparant</u> tape   **J** <u>breakable</u> vase

   G wise <u>consumer</u>   **K** All correct

   H <u>previous</u> meeting

GO

Directions: For numbers 19–24, mark the letter of the word or group of words that belongs in the blank and shows correct capitalization and/or punctuation.

19 **Approximately two-thirds of _____ surface is water.**

   A earths   **C** Earth's

   B Earths'   **D** earth's

20 **This map shows natural features such as**

   F mountains, deserts rivers and oceans.

   G mountains, deserts, rivers, and oceans.

   H mountains, deserts, rivers and, oceans.

   J mountains deserts rivers, and oceans.

21 **Some animal species are extinct because of natural _____ others are threatened with extinction because of people.**

   A forces;   **C** forces,

   B forces: **D** forces

22 **_____ did you know that there are 20,000 species of ants?**

   F Danny;   **H** "Danny,"

   G Danny!   **J** Danny,

23 **_____ a car must have a special device to remove the chemicals from the exhaust before it comes out of the tailpipe.**

   A In our "country"

   B In Our Country,

   C In our Country:

   D In our country,

24 **A group of students interviewed officials _____ Concerned Citizens Committee.**

   F at a local power plant several factories, and the riverdale

   G at a local power plant, several factories, and the Riverdale

   H at a local, power plant, several factories and the Riverdale

   J at a local power plant several Factories, and the Riverdale

GO

Directions: For questions 25 and 26, mark the letter of the sentence with correct punctuation and/or capitalization.

25

A "Do you know anything about global warming?" Asked Jason.

B "That's the increase in Earth's temperature," replied Andrea.

C Lisa added "it's happening because of a buildup of certain gases in the atmosphere."

D Jason was curious to know, "How long the problem has existed?"

26

F Acid rain is a form of pollution, it is caused by chemicals released into the air.

G The chemicals mix with moisture and particles in the air, and create acids.

H Do you know what happens? When it rains or snows.

J Many lakes are so acidic that fish can no longer live in them. Trees in the Appalachian Mountains have also been affected.

Directions: For questions 27–29, mark the letter of the answer that shows correct punctuation and capitalization. Mark the letter for "Correct as is" if the underlined part is correct.

27 **"Can you come to the meeting <u>tonight asked</u> Greg.**

A tonight," Asked

B tonight?" asked

C tonight." Asked

D Correct as is

28 **A speaker will be coming from <u>columbus ohio</u>**

F columbus, Ohio.

G "Columbus" Ohio.

H Columbus, Ohio.

J Correct as is

29 **Our student environmental group may be <u>small but</u> it is very effective.**

A small but,   **C** small, but

B small. But   **D** Correct as is

GO

Directions: For questions 30 and 31, mark the letter of the sentence that is correctly written.

30 **F** Has you heard the Rockets' latest album?

G Mike says that it's their best one yet.

H Well, I don't care for none of the new songs.

J I think their last album was much more better.

31 **A** Meg and I seen an accident on the way to school this morning.

B The driver of a small sports car run a stop sign and hit a pickup truck.

C Fortunately, neither of the drivers was hurt.

D You shoulda seen the front end of the car.

Directions: For questions 32–35, mark the letter of the word that correctly completes the sentence.

32 The boy to _____ you spoke is my older brother.

F who

G whose

H which

J whom

33 As we read the article, we began to better _____ why the problem is so complex.

A understand

B understanding

C understood

D understands

34 Mary and Jake were upset with _____ when they realized their mistake.

F theirselves

G themselves

H himself

J ourselves

35 Mr. Bork asked _____ to play a duet today.

A we

B I

C they

D us

GO

Directions: For questions 36–39, mark the correct word to replace the underlined word.

36 **Wherever you are ready, we can leave.**

F Whenever

G Whether

H Although

J Correct as is

37 **The frightened kitten scurried besides the bed to hide.**

A before

B under

C between

D Correct as is

38 **We purchased a new car soon.**

F before

G recently

H monthly

J Correct as is

39 **Ouch! I hurt my big toe.**

A Indeed

B Hooray

C Whoopee

D Correct as is

Directions: For questions 40 and 41, find the choice that best combines the sentences.

40 **My brother delivers papers. He delivers papers every morning. He delivers papers before school.**

F My brother delivers papers every morning before school.

G Every morning my brother before school delivers papers.

H Before school my brother delivers papers every morning.

J Delivering papers every morning before school is what my brother does.

41 **Please put away the toolbox. The toolbox is on the back porch.**

A The toolbox that is on the back porch, please put it away.

B Please put away the toolbox, the toolbox that is on the back porch.

C Please put away the toolbox on the back porch.

D On the porch is the toolbox to put away please.

STOP

Directions: Read the paragraph about something one student did that had a number of effects.

I meant to do my homework during the weekend, but I got busy and forgot. By the time I realized what had happened, I was staring at my watch at nine o'clock on Sunday night. Because I didn't set my priorities and realize what was important, I didn't finish all of my assignments. Because I didn't finish all of my assignments, my mom wouldn't let me go to soccer practice. Next time, I'm going to write myself a note to remind me to get my homework done on time.

Directions: Now think of a time when something you did caused specific effects, such as doing a science experiment and seeing the results or caring for plants and watching them grow. Write your own paragraph to tell about a cause and its effect, and explain why the cause resulted in the effect.

_____

_____

_____

_____

_____

_____

_____

_____

_____

_____

_____

_____

_____

GO

Directions: Read the letter below. In the letter, a boy explains to his classmates why they should elect him class president.

To my fellow students,

    I'm running for class president because I have many ideas to make our class and our school better. I will talk personally to each one of you to hear what you think. I will share your ideas with the teachers. I will research places in the community where we can go for interesting field trips, and I will do my best to get better food into our lunchroom. A vote for me is a vote for the best school year ever!

                Sincerely,
                Tom

Directions: Now think of something you would like to persuade someone to do. Write a letter to that person explaining why they should do what you want them to. Convince the reader to believe as you do.

_____

_____

_____

_____

_____

_____

_____

_____

_____

_____

_____

STOP

UNIT 3

Final Test
Mathematics

Mathematics

0:50
Pages 140–148
Time Limit:
approx. 50 minutes

SAMPLE A

$(8 + 3) - 5 =$

- **A** 5
- **B** 7
- **C** 0
- **D** 16
- **E** None of these

SAMPLE B

342
$\times\ 6$

- **F** 2042
- **G** 1852
- **H** 2052
- **J** 1842
- **K** None of these

---

1 $(12 - 8) + 9 =$

- **A** 29
- **B** 13
- **C** 5
- **D** 12
- **E** None of these

2   8282
$\times\ 15$

- **F** 828,215
- **G** 123,240
- **H** 134,230
- **J** 124,230
- **K** None of these

3 $105\overline{\smash{\big)}740}$

- **A** 5 R7
- **B** 7 R5
- **C** 6 R5
- **D** 6 R7
- **E** None of these

4 $9 \times \frac{3}{4} =$

- **F** 3
- **G** $6\frac{3}{4}$
- **H** $6\frac{1}{4}$
- **J** $7\frac{1}{4}$
- **K** None of these

5 $7.698 - 5.14 =$

- **A** 12.838
- **B** 1.558
- **C** 2.67
- **D** 2.558
- **E** None of these

6 $\frac{1}{5} + \frac{7}{50} =$

- **F** $\frac{17}{50}$
- **G** $\frac{3}{25}$
- **H** $\frac{4}{25}$
- **J** $\frac{3}{50}$
- **K** None of these

GO

SAMPLE C Sergio spent $3.80 on heavy duty string for his project. He bought 20 feet of string. Which number sentence could you use to find out the price per foot of the string?

A $3.80 + 20 = ☐

B $3.80 − 20 = ☐

C $3.80 × 20 = ☐

D $3.80 ÷ 20 = ☐

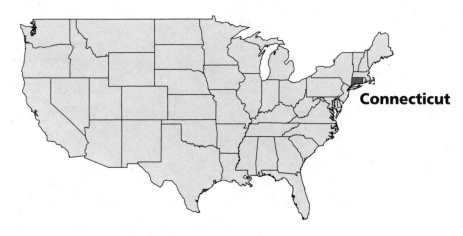

Connecticut

Summer School

Directions: Todd and Melanie received scholarships to attend an eight-week summer program at a school in Connecticut. Do numbers 7–11 about the program.

7 Two-sevenths of the students in the program arrived Sunday afternoon. Three-sevenths of the students arrived Sunday evening. What fraction of the students arrived on Sunday?

A $\frac{6}{49}$

B $\frac{5}{14}$

C $\frac{5}{7}$

D $\frac{1}{7}$

8 At the school store, Todd bought 6 pens for 59¢ each and 8 pencils for 19¢ each. How much did he spend all together?

F $506.00

G $50.60

H $5.06

J $0.506

K None of these

GO

9   The Mathematics Building is 68.3 feet from the Computer Center. The Library is 5 times farther from the Computer Center than the Mathematics Building. What is the distance from the Computer Center to the Library?

A   3415.0 feet

B   341.5 feet

C   73.3 feet

D   13.66 feet

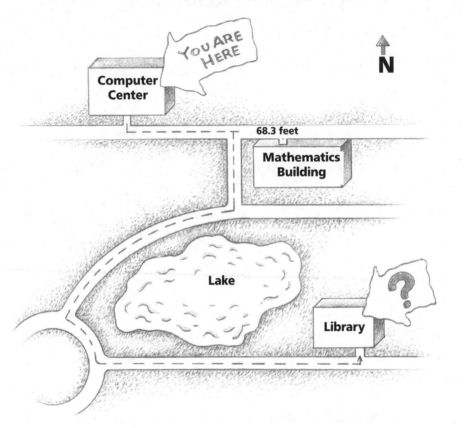

10   Todd traveled 1378 miles from Florida to Connecticut. Melanie traveled 3095 miles from California to Connecticut. How many more miles did Melanie have to travel than Todd?

F   1717 mi

G   2717 mi

H   1727 mi

J   1617 mi

11   Todd, Melanie, and two of their friends went out for dessert and soft drinks. Their bill was $23.40. If the four students shared the cost evenly, how much did each person have to pay?

A $3.90

B $4.68

C $5.75

D   None of these

GO

Quilting Bee

Directions: Rose makes quilts at the Thursday quilting bee each week.
Do numbers 12–14 about Rose's craft.

12 Which pieces of material should Esther use to make the design missing from this pattern?

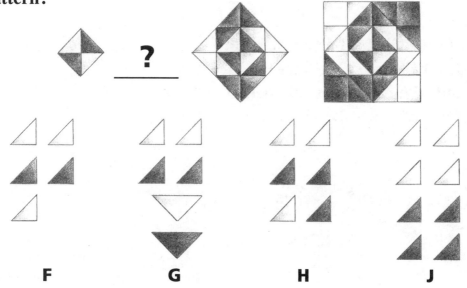

13 Louise put the four pieces below together edge to edge to make a new shape. Which of these could be the shape she made?

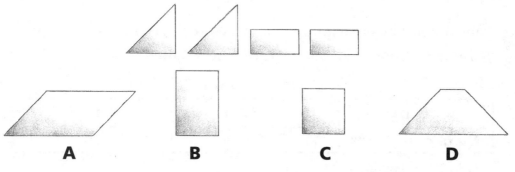

14 The grid shows the green area of one quilted square. Which of these numbers does not describe the shaded part of the grid?

F $\frac{2}{3}$ **H** $\frac{33}{100}$

G 33%   **J** 0.33

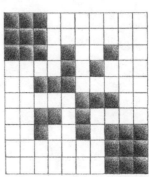

GO

15 How many of the numbers in the box are common multiples of 3 and 8?

A 2   C 4

B 3   D 5

| 6 | 16 | 24 | 32 | 96 |

16 The scale to the right is balanced. All the figures with the same shape have the same weight. Which of the scales below is also balanced?

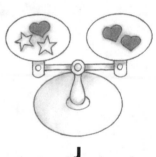

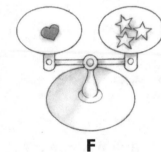   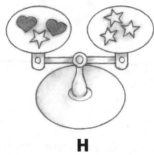   

F   G   H   J

17 Elliott spun the arrow on a spinner 30 times. The results are shown in the table. Which of these spinners did Elliott most likely spin?

Shape	D	H	S	Total Spins
Number of Times	11	10	9	30

A   B   C   D

GO

Directions: Find the correct answer to solve each problem.

18

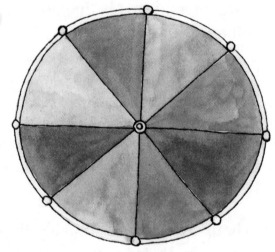

What is the probability of landing on a red section?

F 1 out of 3

G 2 out of 8

H 5 out of 8

J 3 out of 8

19 **What is the square root of 49?**

A 2,401

B 98

C 24.5

D 7

20 **Which shape is not a polygon?**

F

G

H

J

21 **What point shows (–4, 6)?**

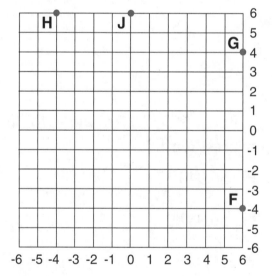

A F

B G

C H

D J

GO

22 **Which number is an improper fraction?**

F 6

G $5\frac{6}{7}$

H $\frac{18}{7}$

J 0.9458

23 **Which figure represents a ray?**

A

B

C ———

D

24 **What is 56,937.17 rounded to the nearest tenth?**

F 56,940.17

G 56,937.2

H 56,937.1

J 56,930

25 **A cube has a side that measures 25 centimeters. What is the total volume of the cube?**

A 15,625 cubic cm

B 625 cubic cm

C 300 cubic cm

D 50 cubic cm

25 centimeters

26 **What percentage of students chose country as their favorite type of music?**

F 80%

G 50%

H 25%

J 12%

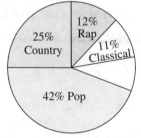

Students' Favorite Types of Music

27 **What fraction shown here is shaded?**

A $\frac{2}{5}$

B $\frac{4}{9}$

C $\frac{9}{4}$

D $\frac{1}{3}$

GO

28 **What is the perimeter of the polygon?**

F 162 millimeters

G 171 millimeters

H 194 millimeters

J 201 millimeters

Side 6: 24 millimeters

Side 1: 28 millimeters

Side 5: 33 millimeters

Side 2: 45 millimeters

Side 4: 54 millimeters

Side 3: 17 millimeters

29 **What is the ratio of students who saw hammerhead sharks to those who saw penguins?**

A 9:14

B 9:43

C 14:9

D 1:2

Animals Seen at the Aquarium

Animal	Number of Students
Sea Lion	6 students
Penguin	14 students
Turtle	11 students
Hammerhead Shark	9 students

30 **Which of the following is a right triangle?**

F

H

G

J

31 **What time does the clock show?**

A 5:39

B 5:37

C 4:37

D 4:34

GO

32 What is the least common denominator of the following fractions: $\frac{3}{2}$, $\frac{5}{12}$

F 24   **H** 12

G 18   **J** 2

33 The population of the world is about 5,927,000,000 people. What digit is in the millions place?

A 2

B 7

C 5

D 9

34 What place does the 8 hold in the number 109,456,321.0894?

F the hundreds place

G the tenths place

H the hundredths place

J the thousandths place

35 Which group of students watch TV for a total of 2 hours?

A Group A

B Group B

C Group C

D Group D

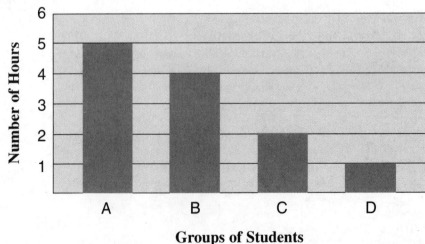

Groups of Students

STOP

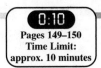

Pages 149–150
Time Limit:
approx. 10 minutes

Social Studies

Final Test
Social Studies

UNIT 4

1 Which place is often called "the cradle of civilization"?

A Persia

B France

C Mesopotamia

D Greece

2 What happened at the end of the Peloponnesian Wars?

F Athens surrendered.

G Greek city-states flourished.

H The Trojan War began.

J The Dark Age ended.

3 How did the Fertile Crescent get its name?

A It was an undiscovered mountain range.

B Its waterway made travel easy.

C It was a center of trade.

D It sat between two rivers and had rich soil.

4 Democracy *most likely* began with

F Babylonian elections.

G American war.

H Greek political ideals.

J Egyptian campaigns.

5 Cuneiform is

A a method of planting.

B a type of writing.

C a style of building.

D a way of distributing.

6 Which body of water would *not* be found on a map of the ancient Middle East?

F Caspian Sea

G Red Sea

H Persian Gulf

J Atlantic Ocean

GO

Directions: Study the map that shows the median age of the U.S. population in 1990, and then do Numbers 7–10.

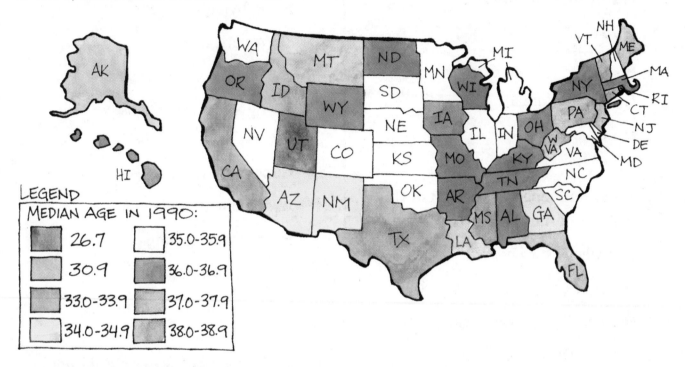

LEGEND
MEDIAN AGE IN 1990:

26.7	35.0-35.9
30.9	36.0-36.9
33.0-33.9	37.0-37.9
34.0-34.9	38.0-38.9

7 Which states had median populations older than 37?

A Arizona and New Mexico

B Alaska and Utah

C Florida and Pennsylvania

D West Virginia and Florida

8 Which state had a median population younger than 33?

F Texas

G Utah

H West Virginia

J Kansas

9 Which two states had the same median age range?

A South Dakota and Virginia

B Rhode Island and Nevada

C Vermont and Georgia

D Iowa and California

10 Which two states were in different median age categories?

F Michigan and South Dakota

G Massachusetts and New York

H Ohio and New Jersey

J Washington and Indiana

STOP

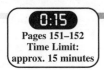

0:15
Pages 151–152
Time Limit:
approx. 15 minutes

Final Test **5**
Science   UNIT

Science

1 The molecule that carries information about traits to be passed from parent to child is called

A CRN.

B DRB.

C DNA.

D CDB.

Directions: Study the chromosome graph, and then do numbers 2–4.

2 **What is it called when a gene does not copy itself exactly?**

F dominant

G albino

H mutation

J camouflage

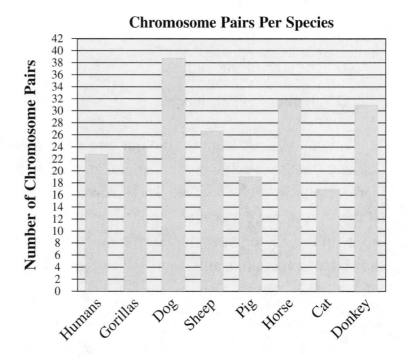

3 **Which species has the most pairs of chromosomes?**

A dog

B pig

C donkey

D human

4 **Given that species with similar numbers of chromosome pairs are quite alike, which pair of species is the most similar?**

F dog and sheep

G horse and donkey

H gorilla and cat

J human and pig

GO

Directions: Read about the experiments, and do numbers 5–7.

Adam wants to find out how lemon juice reacts when it is combined with different substances. In three separate paper cups, he puts equal amounts of baking soda, salt, and sugar. Then he puts 3 drops of lemon juice into each cup. After 30 seconds, he observes all three cups.

5 What is the variable in this experiment?

A the lemon juice

B the time passed

C the size of the cup

D the type of substance

Lily and Corey want to find out how heat, color, and temperature are related. They line one shoebox with white paper and another with black paper. Then they put a thermometer in each shoebox. They place both shoeboxes outside in the sun for one hour. At the start of the experiment, the temperature in both boxes was 72°F. After one hour, the box with the white paper showed a temperature of 85°F, and the box with the black paper showed a temperature of 92°F.

6 What conclusion can Lily and Corey make?

F The color of the paper had no effect on the temperature in the box.

G The black paper absorbed more heat than the white paper.

H The white paper absorbed more heat than the black paper.

J One of the thermometers was broken.

7 Which element would make the best addition to their experiment?

A a shoebox with no lining paper and a thermometer

B a shoebox with extra black paper but no thermometer

C a shoebox with a lid

D a shoebox filled with sand and covered with black paper

STOP

Grade 6 Answer Key

Page 26
1. B
2. F
3. C
4. G
5. C
6. F

Page 28
1. B
2. H
3. D
4. G
5. A
6. J
7. D
8. F

Page 30
1. A
2. B
3. A
4. B
5. B
6. A
7. A
8. B
9. A
10. A

Page 32
1. D
2. A
3. B
4. C
5. H
6. J
7. F
8. G
9. B
10. C
11. D
12. A
13. G
14. H
15. J
16. F
17. A
18. C
19. D
20. B

Page 34
1. C
2. F
3. D
4. J
5. D
6. H
7. B
8. F
9. B
10. F

Page 36

FIRST QUESTION: The author's purpose for writing this passage is to inform the reader about a permanent space laboratory, called International Space Station. I know this because the passage begins talking about it, and several details are provided about the space station.

SECOND QUESTION: The topic sentence of this passage is the first sentence: Do you think it might be cool to live in outer space one day?

THIRD QUESTION: Responses will vary. Possible response: The space station is being built so that experiments can be conducted and so that scientists might be able to find out what we need to live in space for long periods of time.

FOURTH QUESTION: Responses will vary.

Page 38
1. B
2. J
3. B
4. G

Grade 6 Answer Key

Page 41
1. B
2. H
3. A
4. G
5. B
6. J

Page 42
7. C
8. G
9. B
10. H
11. B

Page 44

FIRST QUESTION:
Responses will vary but should include a description of the character and examples of how he or she is compassionate.

SECOND QUESTION: Responses will vary but should include description examples to support the student's answer on whether there is too much violence on TV, in the movies, and in video games.

Page 46
1. D
2. G
3. D

Page 48
1. D
2. J
3. B
4. H

Page 50
1. C
2. J
3. A
4. H

Page 52
1. C
2. J
3. A
4. G

Page 54
1. C
2. H
3. C
4. G

Page 56
1. B
2. J
3. D
4. H

Page 58
1. A
2. F
3. C
4. H
5. D
6. F

Page 60
1. B
2. F
3. A
4. J
5. B
6. H

Page 62
1. B
2. G
3. B
4. H
5. C
6. G

Page 64
1. D
2. J
3. A
4. G
5. D
6. F

Page 68
1. D
2. H
3. D
4. F

Page 69
5. D
6. F

Page 72
1. A
2. J
3. D
4. G

154

Grade 6 Answer Key

A. D
B. G

Page 81
1. B
2. G
3. A
4. H

Page 82
5. C
6. F

Page 84
7. C

Page 85
8. H
9. A
10. G

Page 86
11. C
12. J
13. B
14. F

Page 87
15. B
16. J

Page 88
C. C

Page 89
17. C
18. G
19. A

Page 90
20. J
21. D
22. H
23. A

Page 91
D. B

Page 92
24. D
25. J

Page 93
26. B
27. H
28. B

Page 94
A. B
1. D
2. F
B. D
3. B
4. G

Page 95
5. B
6. F
7. D
8. H
9. C
10. J

Page 96
C. B
11. D
12. H
D. D
13. B
14. H

Page 97
15. A
16. G
17. D
18. G
19. C
20. F

Page 98
E. A
21. B
22. J
23. C
F. E
24. D
25. F

Page 99
FIRST QUESTION: Responses will vary but should tell who is the main character and what he or she is like.

SECOND QUESTION: Responses will vary but should describe the setting of the story.

THIRD QUESTION: Responses will vary but should describe the problem of the main character and how he or she will solve it.

FOURTH QUESTION: Responses will vary.

Grade 6 Answer Key

Page 100
Responses will vary but should compare and contrast two items using the words *same, like, different, unlike, but,* and *however.*

Page 101
- **G.** A
- **26.** C
- **27.** J
- **H.** E
- **28.** C
- **29.** G
- **30.** C

Page 102
- **31.** G
- **32.** D
- **33.** H
- **34.** A
- **35.** J
- **36.** B

Page 103
- **37.** H
- **38.** D
- **39.** H
- **40.** D
- **41.** J
- **42.** A
- **43.** H

Page 104
Responses will vary.

Page 105
- **A.** C
- **B.** K
- **1.** D
- **2.** F
- **3.** A
- **4.** G

Page 106
- **C.** C

Page 107
- **5.** D
- **6.** F
- **7.** D

Page 108
- **8.** F
- **9.** B
- **10.** G

Page 109
- **11.** C
- **12.** G
- **13.** B

Page 110
- **14.** J
- **15.** A
- **16.** J

Page 111
- **D.** D
- **17.** E
- **18.** G
- **19.** A
- **20.** J
- **21.** B

Page 112
- **E.** C
- **22.** C
- **23.** J

Page 113
- **24.** C
- **25.** G
- **26.** D

Page 114
- **27.** G
- **28.** D
- **29.** H
- **30.** C
- **31.** J
- **32.** D
- **33.** J

Page 115
- **1.** A
- **2.** G
- **3.** D
- **4.** H

Page 116
- **5.** D
- **6.** F
- **7.** A
- **8.** H
- **9.** C
- **10.** G

Page 117
- **11.** C
- **12.** J
- **13.** B
- **14.** G

Grade 6 Answer Key

Page 118
15. D
16. F
17. D
18. G

Page 119
1. C
2. J
3. A
4. J
5. B
6. H

Page 120
7. D
8. G
9. A
10. G
11. C
12. G

Page 121
13. C
14. F
15. A
16. H

Page 122
17. A
18. H
19. B
20. J

Page 125
A. D
1. B

Page 126
2. G
3. D
4. F

Page 127
5. B
6. G

Page 128
7. B
8. F
9. D

Page 129
10. F
11. A
12. J
13. C
14. H

Page 130
15. A
16. F
17. C
18. J
19. C
20. A
21. D
22. B
23. G
24. F
25. H
26. J

Page 131
A. C
1. D
B. D
2. F
3. D
4. F

Page 132
5. A
6. H
7. D
8. F
9. C
10. G

Page 133
11. B
12. J
13. D
14. G
15. E
16. F
17. C
18. F

Page 134
19. C
20. G
21. A
22. J
23. D
24. G

Page 135
25. B
26. J
27. B
28. H
29. C

Grade 6 Answer Key

Page 136
30. G
31. C
32. J
33. A
34. G
35. D

Page 137
36. F
37. B
38. G
39. D
40. F
41. C

Page 138
Responses will vary but should describe a cause and its effect and explain why the cause resulted in the effect.

Page 139
Responses will vary but should try and persuade someone to do something and to believe as he or she does about it.

Page 140
A. E
B. H
1. B
2. J
3. B
4. G
5. D
6. F

Page 141
C. D
7. C
8. H

Page 142
9. B
10. F
11. D

Page 143
12. J
13. A
14. F

Page 144
15. A
16. J
17. B

Page 145
18. J
19. D
20. F
21. C

Page 146
22. H
23. B
24. G
25. A
26. H
27. B

Page 147
28. J
29. A
30. H
31. C

Page 148
32. J
33. B
34. H
35. C

Page 149
1. C
2. F
3. D
4. H
5. B
6. J

Page 150
7. D
8. G
9. A
10. H

Page 151
1. C
2. H
3. A
4. G

Page 152
5. D
6. G
7. A

McGraw-Hill Children's Publishing

All our workbooks meet school curriculum guidelines and correspond to
The McGraw-Hill Companies classroom textbooks.

SPECTRUM SERIES

SPECTRUM WORKBOOKS FEATURING MERCER MAYER'S LITTLE CRITTER® GRADES K–2

The nation's premier educational publisher for grades K–12, together with the well-known Mercer Mayer's Little Critter® characters, represents a collaboration of two highly respected "institutions" in the fields of education and children's literature. Like other Spectrum titles, the length, breadth and depth of the activities in these workbooks enable children to learn a variety of skills about a single subject.

- Mercer Mayer's Little Critter family of characters has sold over 100 million books. These wholesome characters and stories appeal to both parents and teachers.

- These entertaining books are based on highly respected McGraw-Hill Companies' textbooks.

- Each book includes easy-to-follow instructions.

NEW! Spelling, Writing, and Language Arts for Grades K–2

- Page counts range from 128–160 full-color pages.

- An answer key is included in each book.

TITLE	ISBN	PRICE
Gr. K - Math	1-57768-800-7	$7.95
Gr. 1 - Math	1-57768-801-5	$7.95
Gr. 2 - Math	1-57768-802-3	$7.95
Gr. K - Reading	1-57768-810-4	$7.95
Gr. 1 - Reading	1-57768-811-2	$7.95
Gr. 2 - Reading	1-57768-812-0	$7.95
Gr. K - Phonics	1-57768-820-1	$7.95
Gr. 1 - Phonics	1-57768-821-X	$7.95
Gr. 2 - Phonics	1-57768-822-8	$7.95
NEW Gr. K - Spelling	1-57768-830-9	$7.95
NEW Gr. 1 - Spelling	1-57768-831-7	$7.95
NEW Gr. 2 - Spelling	1-57768-832-5	$7.95
NEW Gr. K - Writing	1-57768-850-3	$7.95
NEW Gr. 1 - Writing	1-57768-851-1	$7.95
NEW Gr. 2 - Writing	1-57768-852-X	$7.95
NEW Gr. K - Language Arts	1-57768-840-6	$7.95
NEW Gr. 1 - Language Arts	1-57768-841-4	$7.95
NEW Gr. 2 - Language Arts	1-57768-842-2	$7.95

MATH
GRADES K–8

This series features easy-to-follow instructions that give students a clear path to success. This series includes comprehensive coverage of the basic skills, helping children master math fundamentals. Most titles have more than 150 full-color pages, including an answer key.

TITLE	ISBN	PRICE
Gr. K - Math *	1-57768-800-7	$7.95
Gr. 1 - Math *	1-57768-801-5	$7.95
Gr. 2 - Math *	1-57768-802-3	$7.95
Gr. 3 - Math	1-57768-403-6	$7.95
Gr. 4 - Math	1-57768-404-4	$7.95
Gr. 5 - Math	1-57768-405-2	$7.95
Gr. 6 - Math	1-57768-406-0	$7.95
Gr. 7 - Math	1-57768-407-9	$7.95
Gr. 8 - Math	1-57768-408-7	$7.95

* Illustrated by Mercer Mayer

READING
GRADES K–6

This full-color series creates an enjoyable reading environment, even for those who find reading challenging. Each book contains interesting content and colorful, compelling illustrations, so children are eager to find out what happens next. Most titles have more than 150 pages, including an answer key.

TITLE	ISBN	PRICE
Gr. K - Reading *	1-57768-810-4	$7.95
Gr. 1 - Reading *	1-57768-811-2	$7.95
Gr. 2 - Reading *	1-57768-812-0	$7.95
Gr. 3 - Reading	1-57768-463-X	$7.95
Gr. 4 - Reading	1-57768-464-8	$7.95
Gr. 5 - Reading	1-57768-465-6	$7.95
Gr. 6 - Reading	1-57768-466-4	$7.95

* Illustrated by Mercer Mayer

Prices subject to change without notice.

PHONICS/WORD STUDY
GRADES K–6

The books in this series provide everything children need to build multiple skills in language. Focusing on phonics, structural analysis, and dictionary skills, this series also offers creative ideas for using phonics and word study skills in language arts. Most titles have more than 200 pages, including an answer key.

TITLE	ISBN	PRICE
Gr. K - Phonics *	1-57768-820-1	$7.95
Gr. 1 - Phonics *	1-57768-821-X	$7.95
Gr. 2 - Phonics *	1-57768-822-8	$7.95
Gr. 3 - Phonics	1-57768-453-2	$7.95
Gr. 4 - Word Study & Phonics	1-57768-454-0	$7.95
Gr. 5 - Word Study & Phonics	1-57768-455-9	$7.95
Gr. 6 - Word Study & Phonics	1-57768-456-7	$7.95

* Illustrated by Mercer Mayer

SPELLING
GRADES K–6

This full-color series links spelling to reading and writing and increases skills in words and meanings, consonant and vowel spellings, and proofreading practice. Over 200 pages. Speller dictionary and answer key included.

TITLE	ISBN	PRICE
Gr. K - Spelling *	1-57768-830-9	$7.95
Gr. 1 - Spelling *	1-57768-831-7	$7.95
Gr. 2 - Spelling *	1-57768-832-5	$7.95
Gr. 3 - Spelling	1-57768-493-1	$7.95
Gr. 4 - Spelling	1-57768-494-X	$7.95
Gr. 5 - Spelling	1-57768-495-8	$7.95
Gr. 6 - Spelling	1-57768-496-6	$7.95

* Illustrated by Mercer Mayer

LANGUAGE ARTS
GRADES K–6

Encourages creativity and builds confidence by making writing fun! Seventy-two four-part lessons strengthen writing skills by focusing on parts of speech, word usage, sentence structure, punctuation, and proofreading. Each level includes a Writer's Handbook at the end of the book that offers writing tips. This series is based on the highly respected SRA/McGraw-Hill language arts series. More than 180 full-color pages.

TITLE	ISBN	PRICE
Gr. K - Language Arts *	1-57768-840-6	$7.95
Gr. 1 - Language Arts *	1-57768-841-4	$7.95
Gr. 2 - Language Arts *	1-57768-842-2	$7.95
Gr. 3 - Language Arts	1-57768-483-4	$7.95
Gr. 4 - Language Arts	1-57768-484-2	$7.95
Gr. 5 - Language Arts	1-57768-485-0	$7.95
Gr. 6 - Language Arts	1-57768-486-9	$7.95

* Illustrated by Mercer Mayer

WRITING
GRADES K–6

Lessons focus on creative and expository writing using clearly stated objectives and pre-writing exercises. Eight essential reading skills are applied. Activities include main idea, sequence, comparison, detail, fact and opinion, cause and effect, and making a point. Over 130 pages. Answer key included.

TITLE	ISBN	PRICE
Gr. K - Writing *	1-57768-850-3	$7.95
Gr. 1 - Writing *	1-57768-851-1	$7.95
Gr. 2 - Writing *	1-57768-852-X	$7.95
Gr. 3 - Writing	1-57768-913-5	$7.95
Gr. 4 - Writing	1-57768-914-3	$7.95
Gr. 5 - Writing	1-57768-915-1	$7.95
Gr. 6 - Writing	1-57768-916-X	$7.95

* Illustrated by Mercer Mayer